JOSÉ COMBLIN

Cry of the Oppressed,
Cry of Jesus

Meditations on Scripture
and Contemporary Struggle

Translated from the Portuguese
by Robert Barr

ORBIS BOOKS
Maryknoll, New York 10545

The Catholic Foreign Mission Society of America (Maryknoll) recruits and trains people for overseas missionary service. Through Orbis Books Maryknoll aims to foster the international dialogue that is essential to mission. The books published, however, reflect the opinions of their authors and are not meant to represent the official position of the society.

Originally published as *O clamor dos oprimidos, o clamor de Jesus* © 1984 by Editora Vozes Ltda, Rua Frei Luís, 100, 25600 Petrópolis, RJ, Brazil

English translation © 1988 by Orbis Books
Published by Orbis Books, Maryknoll, NY 10545
Manufactured in the United States of America
All rights reserved

Library of Congress Cataloging-in-Publication Data

Comblin, Joseph, 1923—
   Cry of the oppressed, cry of Jesus.

   Translation of: O clamor dos oprimidos, o clamor
de Jesus.
   Includes index.
   1. Liberation theology.   2. Jesus Christ—Person and
offices.   I. Title.
BT83.57.C65315   1987   230′.2   87-24029
ISBN 0-88344-613-8 (pbk.)

Contents

Editor's Note

This book contains Comblin's text (chapters 1–3) and an appendix of scripture passages that are about the cry of the oppressed. The scripture passages in the appendix are divided into three sections, each of which corresponds to one of the chapters in the text—the first group of passages is about the cry of the Israelites that is expressed in the Old Testament; the second is about the cry of Jesus; the third is about the cry of the people of God throughout history and up to the present. There are various ways to use the appendix. Individual readers or groups can first read the text of a chapter and then read corresponding scripture passages in the appendix as a way of deepening reflection on Comblin's themes. It is also helpful to read the scripture passages for a chapter first, reflect on and discuss them, and then turn to Comblin's text as a source of further comment on the themes raised in the citations. A prominent theme that runs through the scripture passages is that in answer to the cry of the oppressed, God raises up human saviors, and those saviors are often drawn from among the ranks of women, the poor, the marginalized.

Introduction

The Letter to the Hebrews is about Jesus' participation in our condition as mortal human beings. It shows us how far Jesus was willing to go in identifying with us in our frailty and afflictions. For "in the days when he was in the flesh, he offered prayers and supplications with loud cries and tears to God, who was able to save him from death . . . " (Heb. 5:7).

This cry of Jesus has a long biblical history. It does not stand alone. No, it is part of a history. It is the echo of the immense cry whose beginning is in the very origins of the people of Israel. And then it grows in volume, multiplying with the multiplication of an immense people that has now covered the earth.

This is a cry, then, that is of the highest importance for the very origins of the history of the people of God. And today, as history comes to a climax, that importance is anything but diminished.

Nor again is the cry merely a literary event. It is not only in the Bible that a people cry. The literary cry of the Bible expresses the real cry of the peoples of the earth, and is recorded in the Bible only because God has given it a key role in the history of human liberation.

In these meditations we shall hear the cry of human beings along their path through history. We shall see that this cry has been, and is, in itself a sign of the liberation that proceeds from God. This is a cry announcing liberation, proclaiming its present reality.

The church in our day has made this cry—which has

seemed to so many to have been stifled—its own, and given it new direction. The cry is addressed to God, but God makes it known to all men and women. The cry is not lost, then. God hears it and then repeats it, transmitting it to the universe of God's creatures; thus God is the interpreter of the cry of God's people.

In chapter 1 we shall examine the origins of Christ's own cry in the history of the people of Israel of bygone times. In chapter 2 we shall hear the cry of Jesus during the time of his passage on earth. And in chapter 3 we shall consider the cry of the people of God in our own time, in the light of the message of the Bible.

Chapter One

The Cry of the Past

DAWN OF LIBERATION

When the people of Israel recorded how they had come to be a people, they could scarcely forget to mention the cry of their forebears. From its origins, Israel was in slavery in Egypt. All of the sons and daughters of Israel toiled in the service of Pharaoh, caught in a desperate situation of oppression. Deprived of all hope, they lacked the strength to break free, to liberate themselves, to escape their implacable fate. Then, at the moment of its most extreme misery, Israel remembered its God, and cried out. That cry mounted to him. And God was moved, and resolved to deliver his people.

The process was threefold, then. There was the oppression, then the cry, then the liberation. And the middle stage was the cry. The cry was the mediator. For God does not act unless moved by a cry. If God's people forget him and fail to call on him, God does not intervene.

All of the "literary traditions" representing the various stages in Israel's reflection on its origins emphasize and hand on the role performed by this cry in the liberation of the people.

The oldest tradition is in the Old Testament passages writ-

3

ten by the "Yahwist." These must have been written during the early years of the monarchy itself, under David or Solomon. It is the most graphic tradition, and reports its facts in the form of a dialogue between Yahweh and Moses.

In those days, Moses used to tend the flocks of his father-in-law. One night, he suddenly saw the burning bush, which did not burn up. Transfixed with astonishment, he heard the Lord calling to him from the midst of the bush. Yahweh revealed himself to Moses that night, and gave him his reason for so doing:

> I have witnessed the affliction of my people in Egypt and have heard their cry of complaint against their slave drivers, so I know well what they are suffering. Therefore I have come down to rescue them from the hands of the Egyptians. . . . So indeed the cry of the Israelites has reached me, and I have truly noted that the Egyptians are oppressing them. Come now! I will send you to Pharaoh to lead my people, the Israelites, out of Egypt [Exod. 3:7–10].

The priestly tradition, which arose after the Babylonian Captivity, the Exile, likewise recalls these happenings in terms of a cry:

> Still the Israelites groaned and cried out because of their slavery. As their cry for release went up to God, he heard their groaning and was mindful of his covenant with Abraham, Isaac, and Jacob [Exod. 2:23–24].

The cry of the people is not just a shout, like the cry of a wild animal, a pure physical reaction. Animals' cries are lost cries. No one hears them. Israel's cry is different. It is addressed to someone: God. God makes a reply. And we have a dialogue between God and human beings.

The people's cry is the cry of someone who refuses simply to submit to oppression. Israel refuses to accept oppression as an inevitable part of its condition. Animals roar, but submit. Their "shout" is not a call for a savior. But the people of God refuse to accept this yoke of theirs, and call out to someone, some judge to do them justice.

Yes, the people's cry is a call for justice. For they refuse to believe that the oppression they suffer can be justice! And so, when they can bear up no longer, they assert their rights before the justice that governs the world. And behold, God intervenes as defender of the people. God acknowledges their dignity and their right to protest—as indeed they have protested—against oppression in the name of their dignity and their rights.

Before intervening, God waits for the people to take cognizance of this dignity of theirs, take cognizance of their human rights. God saves them only when they want to be saved.

Whence such preeminent value, such power, in the cry of this people? Is it not because God is the ultimate source of the cry? This is what Paul will say, in the New Testament, about the cry uttered by God's new people. Now, if the Spirit of God is at the origin of the shout of the new people of God, who come forth from Jesus Christ, is it not perhaps this same Spirit who originated the shout of the ancient people who were making ready for the coming of Christ? Yes, indeed, the people of Israel burst into this great cry because the Spirit of God aroused in them a consciousness, an awareness of their situation, their situation of injustice, and inspired in them a confidence in the liberating will of God. God answered their call because he had been its initiator. He had heard the voice of his own Spirit. He was loyal to himself. And when he gave his sons and daughters, the men and women of Israel, the gift of speech, he could recognize, in their cry, the accents of his own voice, the voice of his blood, his family—the voice of his own.

From what we observe, then, this great cry making itself heard on the earth is the voice of God protesting the unjust oppression of his own people.

Because it comes forth from God, the people's cry proclaims its own response: the promise of liberation. And the Bible is witness of the power of the cry of the poor—a cry that has such force because it contains God's promise.

The biblical narratives, of course, propound God's presence at the heart of the world vividly and suggestively, in images. By means of inspired pictures, those narratives furnish the secret of the discovery of the signs of God's intervention in history. The purpose of the narratives of the cry of God's people is the manifestation of God's promises. In actual reality, God does not appear in the way that the biblical authors narrate the events. Their recitals set forth events in such a way that for some—unbelievers—they remain incomprehensible and irrelevant, while for others—believers—they are full of meaning. For the casual observer, then, these cries have no value, no power. They are but bothersome noises. But casual observers take care that these cries not disturb their tranquillity.

For such people, these cries are merely signs of a bad upbringing. People emit them when they are ignorant and ill-bred. The indifferent fail to recognize the voice of God in these cries—the promises of deliverance that God has made his people. But in reality these cries have the value of promises. They are inspired of God. God himself intends to intervene in history, delivering, liberating, an oppressed people who cry out for salvation.

And just as for some these cries are but unpleasant noises, for others they are the voice of God promising rescue. The Bible strengthens the faith of believers. It confirms, it bears witness to the fact that these cries are part of the history of liberation—the visible part of God's grand design of deliverance.

THE RIGHT TO CRY OUT

The cry of the victim of injustice is so intimately bound up with the life and awareness of the people of Israel that it has entered into their laws. When persons see themselves strangled by a situation of extreme oppression—helpless before the oppressor's might—they still have the ultimate dignity of one last right: the right to cry out to God. And God hears those who cry out for justice. God becomes the defender of those who no longer have anyone to defend them.

Now, who in Israel could be more exposed to injustice and exploitation than the widow or the orphan? When the head of the family, who is also the defender of the family, dies, his widow and children see themselves at the mercy of unscrupulous attackers. These invade their lands, and appropriate their goods and home. If there is no one to defend them in God's name, widows and orphans end up as victims of lying, intrigue, and violence.

Accordingly, the oldest set of laws in Israel, the Code of the Covenant, prescribes:

You shall not wrong any widow or orphan. If ever you wrong them and they cry out to me, I will surely hear their cry. My wrath will flare up, and I will kill you with the sword; then your own wives will be widows, and your children orphans [Exod. 22:21–23].

God's warning is addressed to the whole people. If they observe in their midst cases like these, in which the people themselves tolerate injustices committed against widows and orphans, the wrath of God will flare up against the entire people. This law, then, imposes a responsibility on the whole people. It is an appeal to an obligation incumbent upon all.

Some may perhaps think: How could God's help serve the cause of widows and orphans? Would God's help be really effective? Ah, but to deny the effectiveness of the divine protection would be to doubt the presence of someone among the people who would take up God's cause. When God says, "You shall not wrong" them, and, "I will surely hear their cry," this is God's call to all of the sons and daughters of Israel—to the conscience of each of them—to attend to their obligation of taking up the defense of the widow victimized by the despoilers. This defense, then, becomes the cause of all. Now the heads of families must defend other people's widows as if they were members of their own families. Ineffective, then, God's help, God's call? When God says that he will "hear their cry," he means *he knows of the existence of defenders* who will rise up among the people.

And so God's promise to "hear the people's cry" is the best defense that ever there could be, wherever there are still believers. The cause of God is the cause of everyone. Once God has committed himself to responsibility for a cause, everyone is committed!

The wise know that it is prudent to obey God's laws. In fact, they know that God can even have need of their help. And so they strive to maintain good relations with God, for fear that, if they fail to heed the cry of the poor, they themselves will be without God's help in their own hour of need. The wise, then, will not foolishly compromise a juridical system that guarantees the Israelites a minimum of security. They would risk destroying a recourse of which they might stand in need themselves one day. If the cry of the poor has no weight with them, they will risk abandonment by God the day God is their only recourse:

> He who shuts his ear to the cry of the poor
> will himself also call and not be heard
> [Prov. 21:13].

CRIES OF THE OPPRESSED, OF THE POOR

The Psalms frequently voice the cry of that most oppressed and despised of peoples, the poor. They call on the witness of past history, the memory of the days when God delivered his people when they had fallen victim to oppression. They express confidence in God and loyalty to him. The poor and oppressed have faith that God will respond. They know that prayers like these will have an effect. And they are not necessarily counting on miracles. They know that their call to God is a call to the people of God, as well. And God does justice through the intermediary of his people. God avenges the poor through the intermediary of his people and of all who take seriously the covenant between Yahweh and his people. Prayer can be public witness!

Later, people's understanding of the Psalms became more "spiritual." Their cries took on the meaning of hope of a future reward. In Christian times, they were interpreted in the light of God's total response: Jesus Christ. For through Christ had come the promised liberation of the oppressed. Still, at first the Psalms really called on God in a juridical system that provided for a call to God as an integral part of its structure.

Let us see how the psalmists raise their voices to the God of liberation in protest against aggression and injustice:

> When I call out to the LORD,
>   he answers me from his holy mountain [Ps. 3:5].

This is the cry of someone persecuted, for that person says:

> O LORD, how many are my adversaries!
>   Many rise up against me! . . .
> But you, O LORD, are my shield;
>   my glory, you lift up your head! [Ps. 3:2,4].

An ancient tradition has it that this prayer is the prayer of David when he was being persecuted by his son Absalom. In itself this tradition is not of much historical worth. But it attests to the confidence of the daughters and sons of Israel. As God saved David, so God could save other persecuted as well. And as God used contingent factors on this occasion in history, so today he will be able to make use of current events, and especially of the fidelity of his people, to avenge unrighteousness and save his just ones who are oppressed:

> I call upon you, for you will answer me, O God;
>> incline your ear to me; hear my word.
>
> Show your wondrous kindness,
>> O savior of those who flee
>> from their foes to refuge at your right hand
>>> [Ps. 17:6–7].

> In my distress I called upon the LORD
>> and cried out to my God;
>
> From his temple he heard my voice,
>> and my cry to him reached his ears [Ps. 18:7].

According to the Second Book of Samuel, Psalm 18 was attributed to David, who was singing his deliverance by God from his oppressors, especially from the hands of Saul (2 Sam. 22:7).

Psalm 22 has been placed on the lips of Jesus on the cross. In this psalm, a just person, who is being persecuted, beseeches God for deliverance, and since this recalls the cries of Israel's forebears, these cries are made the basis of the psalmist's confidence that God will act in this situation too:

> In you our fathers trusted;
>> they trusted, and you delivered them.

To you they cried and they escaped;
in you they trusted, and they were not put to
shame [Ps. 22:5–6].

For he has not spurned nor disdained
the wretched man in his misery.
Nor did he turn his face away from him,
but when he cried out to him, he heard him
[Ps. 22:25].

And other psalms say:

To you, O LORD, I call;
O my Rock, be not deaf to me,
Lest, if you heed me not,
I become one of those going down into the pit
[Ps. 28:1].

Yet you heard the sound of my pleading
when I cried out to you [Ps. 31:23].

When the afflicted man called out, the LORD
heard,
and from all his distress he saved him [Ps. 34:7].

When the just cry out, the LORD hears them,
and from all their distress he rescues them
[Ps. 34:18].

The cry of the persecuted is the central theme of two more
psalms as well, Psalm 88 and Psalm 107:

O LORD, my God, by day I cry out;
at night I clamor in your presence.

Let my prayer come before you;
    incline your ear to my call for help. . . .
Daily I call upon you, O LORD;
    to you I stretch out my hands. . . .
But I, O LORD, cry out to you . . .
                    [Ps. 88:2–3,10,14].

They cried to the LORD in their distress;
    from their straits he rescued them [Ps. 107:6].

And this last verse is repeated, like a refrain, throughout Psalm 107: in verses 13, 19, and 28. This psalm celebrates God's help to the poor in the midst of their afflictions.

Yahweh is so identified with his people that they have no hesitation in calling for his intercession in time of affliction. God has committed himself, and helps them in an efficacious way. Thus the cries of these prayers were the people's right, to be exercised in their daily lives, whenever they found themselves in desperate straits. The theme of the cry was such a key one that it became part of Israel's heritage, and, as we see, there were even passages that the Israelites could use word-for-word when they wanted to call on God.

ISRAEL'S CRY IN HISTORY

The authors of the historical books of the Old Testament wrote at moments when a great number of God's people, especially those in authority—kings, functionaries, and military officials—were more concerned with economic power and armed might than with religion and God. They trusted more in their own strength than in the power of God. They devoted themselves to a policy of force, and sought to imitate their more powerful neighbors, whom they took as their inspiration and model. They sighed for a strong state. This, they were sure, would be their best warranty against catastrophe.

Now, it happened, this policy of force was implemented at the expense of the people, especially the poor. The poor had to supply the king, the functionaries, and the army with the needed resources. Once it was put in practice, the politics of force subjected the people to a yoke that could be compared only with the one imposed on them by Pharaoh long ago. It is easy to see, then, why the people's cry to Yahweh in a moment of oppression was scarcely looked on with favor by the people's leaders! After all, now it was they who were the oppressors, not Pharaoh. And so the cry became an act of subversion.

Faced with this politics of force, the inspired prophetic authors who were writing the past history of Israel celebrated the bygone time of the so-called Judges, when there was no king, no bureaucracy, and no standing army, and when the people could simply cry to Yahweh and Yahweh would save them from their enemies.

In those times the people relied on themselves, not on kings. They had confidence that, at the right moment, God would raise up the needed leaders. But these leaders remained in power only as long as was necessary, and had no army of their own, nor any bureaucracy. Thus the people had only themselves to rely on—and Yahweh's might—to solve their problems. And of course they knew they could count on Yahweh because they had struck a covenant with him, a permanent alliance, and it surely would not fail them at the moment help was needed. Thus had Yahweh enabled the people to save themselves without the help of kings, whose domination now weighed so heavily upon them.

This was what had happened when Israel fell to the power of the Edomites. According to the sacred writer, the reason for Israel's defeat had been its infidelities.

But when the Israelites cried out to the LORD, he raised up for them a savior, Othniel, son of Caleb's younger brother Kenaz, who rescued them. The spirit of the LORD came upon him, and he judged Israel. When he went out to war, the LORD delivered Cushanrishathaim, King of Aram, into his power, so that he made him subject [Judges 3:9–10].

Later, Israel was eighteen years under the domination of the Moabites. Again the Israelites cried out to Yahweh, and again Yahweh raised up for them a savior—Ehud, son of Gera, of the tribe of Benjamin (Judges 3:15). And Ehud liberated his people from Moabite domination, slaying their king and vanquishing them in battle.

Another time, Israel was oppressed by the Canaanites. "But the Israelites cried out to the LORD" (Judges 4:3), and God sent them Deborah, who took charge of the war of liberation of God's people.

Now the people fell into the hands of the Midianites. Life was indeed hard for them then:

Thus was Israel reduced to misery by Midian, and so the Israelites cried out to the LORD. When Israel cried out to the LORD because of Midian, he sent a prophet to the Israelites, who said to them, "The LORD, the God of Israel, says: I led you up from Egypt; I brought you out of the place of slavery. I rescued you from the power of Egypt and of all your other oppressors. I drove them out before you and gave you their land. And I said to you: I, the LORD, am your God; you shall not venerate the gods of the Amorites in whose land you are dwelling. But you did not obey me" [Judges 6:6–10].

The people were unwilling to credit the words of this prophet. Then Yahweh sent Gideon to them. And Gideon managed to convince a part of the people, deliver the oppressed people, and reestablish the covenant with Yahweh.

The same thing occurred in the time of Jephthah. This time the Israelites were subjugated and abased by the Philistines and Ammonites.

> Then the Israelites cried out to the LORD, "We have sinned against you; we have forsaken our God and have served the Baals." The LORD answered the Israelites: "Did not the Egyptians, the Amorites, the Ammonites, the Philistines, the Sidonians, the Amalekites, and the Midianites oppress you? Yet when you cried out to me, and I saved you from their grasp, you still forsook me and worshiped other gods. Therefore I will save you no more. Go and cry out to the gods you have chosen; let them save you now that you are in distress." But the Israelites said to the LORD, "We have sinned. Do to us whatever you please. Only save us this day" [Judges 10:10–15].

Then the Israelites discarded all of the religious paraphernalia of the other gods, and Yahweh sent them Jephthah.

There can be litte doubt, from what we have seen, that the cry to Yahweh constituted a basic institution in Israel. It replaced the strong state, the military state. The foundation of Israel's resistance in its political difficulties was its unity and its loyalty to its specific vocation and calling. But the moment Israel allowed itself to be corrupted by its neighbors, it immediately lost its identity, specificity, and unity, and fell victim to oppressors. The remedy prescribed by the prophets was loyalty to Yahweh, and confidence in Yahweh. It was in Yahweh, then, that the people always found the means of which they had need in order to save themselves. A king was superfluous.

WHEN GOD DOES NOT HEAR THE CRY

The last case presented in the Book of Judges shows us that there are times when God is not disposed to hear the cry of his people. The Books of Samuel and of the prophets offer a variety of such cases, and give the reason for each. For example, God may fail to heed his people's cry because they have broken the covenant, or because they have staked their welfare on a policy of armed might. Thus when Israel dares to give itself to the service of foreign gods, who foster, legitimate, and sacralize a policy of military expansionism and power, God forsakes his covenant. God declines to comply with the clauses of the contract.

This was precisely what happened when the people first demanded a king. What they really wanted in a king was a military politics, a policy of war and conquest. They sought a permanent leader and an army to undertake new military campaigns. They had decided to enter the race for power and dominion in the Middle East.

Then Yahweh said, "I refuse to play this game. Will you have a king? Fine. Then here is a king. But count on me no longer." God sent Samuel to the israelites to communicate this denunciation. And Samuel told the Israelites:

The rights of the king who will rule you will be as follows: He will take your sons and assign them to his chariots and horses, and they will run before his chariot. He will also appoint from among them his commanders of groups of a thousand and of a hundred soldiers. He will set them to do his plowing and his harvesting, and to make his implements of war and the equipment of his chariots. He will use your daughters as ointment-makers, as cooks, and as bakers. He will take the best of your fields, vineyards, and olive groves, and give them

to his officials. He will tithe your crops and your vineyards, and give the revenue to his eunuchs and his
slaves. He will take your male and female servants, as
well as your best oxen and your asses, and use them to do
his work. He will tithe your flocks and you yourselves
will become his slaves. When this takes place, you will
complain against the king whom you have chosen, but
on that day the LORD will not answer you [1 Sam. 8:11–
18].

Everything Samuel is describing concerning the domination exercised by the new king reflects Israel's historical experience. The Books of Samuel and the Book of Judges are
nothing but a commentary on this prophecy of Samuel. The
military policy incarnated in the king, and chosen by Israel,
comes with a huge "price tag": the domination detailed by
Samuel in his prophecy. From being a free people, Israel
becomes a slave people, under the yoke of the military leader
they themselves have chosen. Faced with this decision on the
part of his people, God refuses to answer them. God no
longer comes to the help of a people caught up in dreams of
political and military grandeur, and bent on violent adven-
ture. God is not the mediator of his people's political problems.

A great deal of light is shed on the history of Christendom
by the theology of the historical books of Israel. How often
Christian peoples have thought that they could count on
Christ in their wars of aggression! True, they always ap-
pealed to motives of legitimate defense as well. But all peoples have always justified their wars of aggression by
appealing to motives of legitimate defense. God did not
agree. And those among the theologians, bishops, and priests
who taught that God did agree—that Christian wars of
aggression were legitimate—deceived us, falsifying the truth.
The God of Jesus Christ does not support—cannot support—

militaristic policies of conquest and expansionism.

Whenever Christians proclaimed that God was on their side in such a war, they lied. They were substituting the gods of the Amorites, Ammonites, and Egyptians for the true God, creating and worshipping an idol. And they were blaspheming the true God, by giving his name to a bloodthirsty idol.

How often the prophets had to speak out to recall these basic truths to mind when the people had been deceived by false prophets!

Jeremiah, for example, had to show the people that they were denying God. He had been sent to communicate to the people that God considered the covenant broken. In Yahweh's eyes Israel had committed breach of covenant when it sought the protection of foreign gods—gods who favored a policy of greatness and power, a policy of developmentalism and expansionism on the part of a dominant class.

A conspiracy has been found, the LORD said to me, among the men of Judah and the citizens of Jerusalem. They have returned to the crimes of their forefathers who refused to obey my words. They also have followed and served strange gods; the covenant which I had made with their fathers, the house of Israel and the house of Judah have broken. Therefore, thus says the LORD: See, I bring upon them misfortune which they cannot escape. Though they cry out to me, I will not listen to them. Then the cities of Judah and the citizens of Jerusalem will go and cry out to the gods to which they have been offering incense. But these gods will give them no help whatever when misfortune strikes [Jer. 11:9–12].

God's refusal to come to the assistance of unfaithful Israel is so adamant that Jeremiah is forbidden to intercede for the people when they have broken the covenant:

Do not intercede on behalf of this people, nor utter a plea for them. I will not listen when they call to me at the time of their misfortune [Jer. 11:14].

The prophet Micah pronounced a violent harangue against the rulers of the people and the whole leading class of Israel:

> They eat the flesh of my people,
>   and flay their skin from them,
>   and break their bones.
> They chop them in pieces like flesh in a kettle,
>   and like meat in a caldron.
> When they cry to the LORD,
>   he shall not answer them;
> Rather shall he hide his face from them at that time,
>   because of the evil they have done [Mic. 3:3–4].

Zechariah presided over a solemn convocation of the whole people upon their return from exile, recalling to them the conditions of the covenant:

Render true judgment, and show kindness and compassion toward each other. Do not oppress the widow or the orphan, the alien or the poor; do not plot evil against one another in your hearts [Zech. 7:9–10].

And Zechariah reminded the people that their forebears had broken these clauses in the covenant. He also reminded them of the outcome:

Then the LORD of hosts in his great anger said that, as they had not listened when he called, so he would not listen when they called . . . [Zech. 7:13].

Actually, the right to call on God is reserved to the poor. When the people embrace notions and policies of power, and themselves become the oppressor, God's part of the pact, too, is broken. Their right to call to God vanishes. Solidarity between God and an earthly power dissolves. Only solidarity between God and the oppressed, the poor, remains in force.

For us—for the Christian church—this right to call on God is of the utmost moment. It gives pastoral theory and practice its orientation, and generally shapes the attitude of the church in the world. For God does not respond to the cry of the poor by means of simple miracles. No, God has chosen his spokespersons, his instruments in this world—human beings. They represent God's interests and carry out his deeds here on earth. These men and women make up God's people, his church. The church is charged with responding in God's name, communicating God's response in some concrete way.

And so when the powerful, the mighty powers, call on God, trusting in him and beseeching his aid, it is the mission of the church to undeceive them, by refusing to foster their illusions or further their abuses and blasphemies, which they commit by falsely invoking God's name. The church must warn them of the evil they are committing. The church must save God's honor, by denouncing mystification, and showing that the god called on in this way is a pagan god, an idol, and that it is blasphemy to use Christian names to invoke a pagan god. The mission of the church is like the missions of Samuel, Jeremiah, Micah, and Zechariah.

And then the church must take up the defense of the poor in the name of God. Actually the church has very little power of its own. Historical circumstances have sometimes lent it power. But its own power is very limited when it comes to the economic or political or cultural sphere. It is not in virtue of any power that it acts in God's name, but in virtue of its authority to issue a call. It has the power to mobilize human beings. It does not act on its own behalf, but summons all the forces of the world to hear the voice of God. Its mission is to cry out with a loud voice, to appeal to everyone for his and her cooperation, to awaken all persons to their responsibility for the rights of the oppressed, the poor. The church is like a loudspeaker, echoing and repeating the words of God to the ends of the earth.

As we see, it is not a matter of automatic effects, as if relations between God and human beings were governed by mechanical forces. There is no automatic response. God's response to the call of the oppressed consists in the action of the church and its prophets, who utter cries of disquietude, concern, and anxiety, and so awaken all human beings to a consciousness of their responsibility and culpability.

This power of mobilization residing in the word of God cannot be weighed mathematically. It is not a military sort of might. That could be measured. God's power cannot be measured. But it is real: it performs tasks. It achieves results.

It is true that God may see his work delayed and limited when he entrusts it to human beings, however excellent his choice of those he sends. But God sends his Spirit, too, and this gives his prophets strength, and his church the necessary graces to carry out this peaceful "general mobilization." If the task fails, the fault is not God's, but that of human beings.

Great is the church's responsibility, then. If it fails to perform its role, by failing to respond adequately to the cry of the poor in God's name, it will bring discredit on God, on Jesus Christ, and on itself. It will lose its titles to respect, lose its raison d'être, and finally unleash a revolt of men and women against God.

It is most regrettable that, in recent centuries, up until the time of Vatican II and Medellín, the church had so often kept silent even though its mission consisted in speaking in the name of God. In modern times bishops and priests were appointed by kings and civil governments, and kings and civil governments were willing to appoint only those who would create no problems for them. Then came resentment on the part of much of society, and a war, covert or overt, between liberal governments and the church. And the church learned to defend its own rights before all else, and thus neglected its true role in the world.

Now the church has begun to learn its role again. It has begun to listen to the cry of the poor to God. Now the church has remembered the response it is to give in the name of God. Now it knows its power of mobilization, and knows it must exercise that power if it is to be totally at the disposition of the Spirit of God. Now it has stood up to speak and to summon, full knowing the cost. The prophets were persecuted precisely because they were unwilling to endorse the mighty undertakings of states, and because they dared to speak in the name of the poor when speaking in the name of the poor was considered subversive. After all, it is of the highest importance to the great powers of this world to be able to count on the energies and service of the poor for their safety and aggrandizement. Thus any cry that the poor might raise against their oppressed condition is regarded as subversive.

Chapter Two

The Cry of Jesus

The cry of the poor and of a people oppressed returns in the gospel more movingly than ever. Jesus, too, was poor and oppressed. He took on the condition of the oppressed, especially in the moment of his great cry—in his moment of his extreme misery and total abandonment. All three Synoptic Evangelists—the writers of the Gospels of Matthew, Mark, and Luke—recount Jesus' cry: that echo of the cry of Israel's poor. The cross had been thrown up; Jesus had been crucified; and his agony was approaching its end. And Saint Matthew says:

> Then toward midafternoon Jesus cried out in a loud tone, "*Eli, Eli, lema sabachthani?*", that is, "My God, my God, why have you forsaken me?" [Matt. 27:46; see Ps. 22:1].

Mark hands on exactly the same tradition (Mark 15:33–34). Matthew, in words echoed by Mark, adds:

> Once again Jesus cried out in a loud voice, and then gave up his spirit [Matt. 27:50; see Mark 15:37].

Luke, altering the tradition, refers to a single cry, and places on Jesus' lips a verse from another psalm:

Jesus uttered a loud cry and said,

"Father, into your hands I commend my spirit"
[Luke 23:46; see Ps. 31:6].

Is there really a connection between Jesus' cry and the cry of the Old Testament people in their oppression? At first glance the relationship does not seem especially evident. But after closer examination it becomes clear that there were not two cries. There was only one, the one we meditated on in chapter one.

Part of the proof of this is that Matthew and Mark could not have been ignorant of the fact that the *particular* cry they attribute to Jesus is a cry from Psalm 22; it is exactly the same cry, in the same words. Mark and Matthew, like their sources, know very well that they are quoting a psalm, and that in his cry on the cross Jesus was praying this psalm. Jesus' cry and the cry of Psalm 22 are complementary, then. What the gospel writers are telling us is that Jesus, an Israelite, uttered this great cry as the last resort, the ultimate right of the oppressed people of Israel and their poor.

It is clear, then, that Israel's great cry was uttered by Jesus on the cross. Thus Israel's cry is of enormous significance both for an understanding of Jesus' own cry, and for the faith and activity of the church.

JESUS AND THE CRY OF HIS PEOPLE

In the Gospels, Jesus is the incarnation of the people of Israel. Matthew's Gospel shows him being taken by his parents while still a baby to Egypt, where he experienced in his own flesh the exile suffered in the past by his people. For it was from Egypt, the psalmist had sung, that the people's liberator would return.

Jesus' cry on the cross is the culmination of the whole cry of Israel, of all of the oppression of his people throughout their history. Jesus has gathered up within himself the whole cry of the oppressed people.

This is the cry that gives Jesus' death and oppression their real meaning. Jesus' death is not an isolated incident, a happening that occurred to one solitary individual. Jesus himself has told us that. Jesus' death is not just one more crime in a long series of isolated, meaningless crimes. If Jesus' death had been simply one more crime, it would have no meaning for the world. But his cry signifies the oppression of his people. In resurrecting the cry of ancient Israel, and of the righteous victims of persecution, Jesus wakes the whole world. For his cry embraces that world.

This is the cry explained in chapter 8 of the Gospel of John, where John describes Jesus' great altercation with the representatives of Israel, the leaders of the people. Jesus denounces their plots against his life. He shows them that the real reason for their scheming is not that they are the offspring of Abraham, or that they are obedient to God, but that all their aspiration is to lies and death—that they are oppressors, and the servants of Satan. Jesus declares that his death will bring Israel's true situation out in the open, for here was a people that had been victimized by lies, murder, and death. Jesus' cry proclaims the oppression through which the people of Israel have had to pass as a result of their breach of their covenant with God.

This cry resounds with a terrible accusation against all the authorities of Israel. It is the denunciation of the situation in which Jesus' people now found themselves—a situation of oppression like that which they had endured in Egypt. The only difference was that now the oppressors were the very leaders of Israel, the experts in the Law, the Pharisees, the priests, and the elders.

Jesus' shout is a shout against the current situation of oppression suffered by his people, a people whom the authorities have sought to crush and stifle. To the authorities, the problem seems different. The scribes complain that the people refuse to submit to their meticulous casuistry. The Pharisees complain that the people lack devotion—that they fail to observe the Sabbath, the customary prayers and good works, the feasts and fasts. The priests complain that sacrifices are no longer offered in the Temple. But all these complaints serve only to distract attention from the true complaint—God's complaint—that there is no justice, no mercy, and that the people are despised and flouted. Jesus cries out in protest against a state of national calamity like that which had occurred when the people were enslaved in Egypt. This situation threatens Israel's survival as people of God. The covenant has been radically violated. The people have been annihilated, made as nothing, by their leaders.

During his ministry as an itinerant preacher, Jesus, seeing the concrete situation of the people, showed his disciples the sad fact: a people without shepherds, scattered sheep, heading nowhere (Matt. 9:36). The shepherds were concerned for their own interests. They had no interest in the sheep.

Jesus also accused the Pharisees and scribes of abusing the Law and their mission as leaders for the purpose of deceiving the people and exercising their dominion over them, and so of repeating the abominations and exploitation of the foreign dominators of times gone by (Matt. 23:4).

But now the moment of total denunciation is at hand. The state of the people's need and abandonment has descended to the extreme, as they suffer annihilation at the hands of the very ones whose mission is to save them. In such a situation, Jesus makes an option for the side of the subjected, the abandoned, the victims of the leaders' irresponsible oppression. Actually, he has been on their side from the start. He has followed the roads that lead to the little towns and villages of Galilee, the remotest region of the land of Israel. There he has met simple folk, the sick, the crippled, the blind, lepers, those possessed by evil spirits, sinners, prostitutes, exploiters of the poor and unemployed. Among the leaders he has observed a mere vestige of religion, cloaking a lack of genuine solidarity, of comprehension of the misfortunes of the people, and a hardness of heart—an insensitivity to God's appeals.

Jesus could see all this because he worked his way in among his people through the doorway of the poor. He perceived the misery that the mighty never sense because it is hidden from eyes that see only the superficial.

And Jesus demonstrated solidarity with his true family, the multitudes of the forsaken. He took them as his new family. He identified with them in such a way that his attitude at once awakened mistrust in the authorities. To these, it seemed evident that Jesus' intent was to uncover what ought to remain concealed, and speak of matters that were better left unmentioned. Jesus was bringing out into the open something no one wanted to see.

When the poor are completely disorganized and scattered, when they lack all opportunity for self-expression, they win only silence and contempt. But when they dare raise their voices, and show themselves, they stir up anger, hatred, and violent reaction. This is what happened to Jesus. Merely by speaking of forbidden subjects, and revealing hidden truths, Jesus was engaging in denunciation. The denunciation did not have to be formulated as such. Jesus' mere solidarity with the crowds was unacceptable.

Now, Jesus took on the condition of the poor and abandoned precisely in order to stir up reaction. He did not take up the life of an oppressed person out of a depraved taste for misery—out of an attraction for the ugly and the horrible.

No, it was not because he enjoyed evil and suffering, or the misery of the sick, the paralyzed, the blind, the sinners, and all those marginalized and abandoned persons in whose midst he chose to dwell. It was because he wanted to be their promise and source of life.

Being their way and source of life led to a way, a path— indeed, he was himself their Way, their Truth, and their Life—of hostility on the part of the authorities, just as his solidarity with the abandoned flocks aroused the wrath of those in charge. But he knew beforehand what their reaction would be. Indeed he sought to provoke it, for he wished to break the silence, and have done with seeming tranquillity and false peace.

Yes, Jesus succeeded in drawing upon himself the full force of the resentment and hatred of the unworthy leaders of the people. He obliged them to show themselves for what they were, and not for what they wished to seem. He obliged them to show themselves in all their truth—as murderers, liars, and consummate traitors to the covenant that they pretended to defend and promote.

And so the forces of oppression, which had been exerted in scattered fashion on the people as a whole, were concentrated now on a single object, and unleashed all their ferocity when Jesus so openly demonstrated his solidarity with the oppressed. Now was fulfilled the prophecy of Isaiah, and to the letter:

> It was our infirmities he bore,
> our sufferings he endured [Matt. 8:17; Isa. 53:4].

Not only did he have compassion on these infirmities, and share them, but he drew upon himself all of the forces that had unleashed them.

On the cross he acknowledged that he had been treated in this way because he had entered by the doorway of the poor, because he had chosen the world of the poor, denouncing what their leaders refused to see. He acknowledged that he had drawn on himself the implacable wrath of his adversaries—that he had made every one of the authorities turn on him. Pilate and Herod had even been reconciled. Yes, the evil-doers had entered into a pact to obliterate him, to reduce him to silence, by the most effective means possible. We have a saying today that might be applied to Jesus, and the anachronism will make no difference: "The best prophet is a dead prophet."

And this is exactly why Jesus can, with full right, take up the cry of the poor—because he has drawn upon himself the oppression of all. In uttering his cry, he is shouting in the name of the whole people of Israel. His cry is the cry of the people. On the cross he performs the ministry of representing a people brought low. He is the incarnation of a people oppressed and rejected by the very ones who ought to have performed the mission of saving them.

In the view of the gospel writers, Jesus represents not only his contemporaries, represents not only the people of Israel, in their history of oppression and humiliation—he represents the poor and oppressed of all time. From the cry of Israel in Egypt until now, all the cries of the oppressed throughout the ages culminate in Jesus' cry on the cross at the moment he expired.

In taking up their cry, Jesus gave the people back their voice. Long had this people lived humiliated and voiceless! And the doctors of the Law explained that this was the people's own fault. They suffered because they were undisciplined, because of the evil they had wrought. And so God had chastised them, punished them, while rewarding their dominators with a prosperity proportioned to their virtues. This is why the people were voiceless. It was the prophets who had been the voice of the people, but it had been long indeed since a prophet had arisen in Israel.

The people no longer even remembered their supreme right as people of God: to call on Yahweh—their right to shout out against the destruction of the covenant, their right to reject their leaders and give their allegiance to others, as they had once rejected the leadership of the Egyptians, and the Babylonians, the Amorites, and Midianites. They had forgotten that they could cry out and God would hear their cry, the cry of the oppressed. They had forgotten that they could exercise the highest right of the daughters and sons of God—the right to beg God for help in their extremity.

In crying to the Father with the cry of the poor, Jesus showed the people the path of dignity again. He showed them that they ought not accept their situation passively, but should remember the rights of the members of the people of God, their right to the solidarity of the whole people in the name of the covenant. They should remember that they were not purely and simply responsible for their misery, but that the cause of the domination to which they were subjected was the breach of the covenant and of their whole social solidarity. They should remember that, when faced with such circumstances, they should denounce to God the injustices afflicting them.

The synoptic tradition contemplates Jesus' cry on the cross in the light of the history of Israel. For Matthew, Mark, and Luke, Jesus' cry on the cross recalled the people's cry in Egypt, and all the adversities of their history. And later, in the days of the Christian church, it grew more and more clear that the history of Israel was as a parable, a parable of the history of the whole of humanity. Israel's fate actually represented the fate of all peoples, who, in the eyes of God, are but a single people.

Israel's oppression neither was nor is unique in the history of humanity. Quite the contrary. It is a portrait of all humanity. Among all peoples the poor are humiliated, marginalized, rejected, and accused of being the cause of the evils that beset them.

And as God hears the cry of his people, so he hears the cry of all of the oppressed of the world. What God has demonstrated in Israel is his attitude toward the whole of humanity. Not only the oppressed of long-ago Israel, but all of the oppressed of the world have the right to call on God—have the right that God hear their cry.

And so Jesus' solidarity is not only with the poor of his people, but with all oppressed humanity. Israel's cry expresses the cry of the oppressed of all times. Israel's cry gives them all a voice, gives them all a way out. God heard Israel's cry. Now God hears the cry of the whole body of the human race.

The Letter to the Hebrews expresses the universalization of Jesus' cry:

> In the days when he was in the flesh, he offered prayers and supplications with loud cries and tears to God, who was able to save him from death, and he was heard because of his reverence. Son though he was, he learned obedience from what he had suffered [Heb. 5:7–8].

Jesus entered into solidarity not just with Israel, but with all God's sons and daughters:

> Jesus likewise had a full share in [our flesh and blood], that by his death he might rob the devil, the prince of death, of his power, and free those who through fear of death had been slaves their whole life long [Heb. 2:14–15].

Jesus wished to learn what it is to be human—wished to know life, wished to know the fear of death, and through that fear, the temptation to slavery. He saw his sisters and brothers captive and timorous their whole life long. And he would not stand for it. He rebelled against the fear. He rejected the terror. He defied death. He challenged death to its face, and thus unshackled himself from the domination of the demon and of all those who serve as his minions. He vanquished fear, and vanquished death, forcing his adversaries to lay down their arms. He sought to know what it was to be concretely human—but he did not accept it. He sought to be human not as human beings actually lived, but as they all should have lived.

As a human being, he had to confront all of the aggression of the powers of death and the lie. Jesus drew upon himself not the oppression of Israel alone, but of all of the poor of the world. Because he represented the Father, he was able to speak both in Israel's name and in that of all of the oppressed of the world.

Thus it was that Jesus presented to his Father the cry of the world, the cry of human beings—the cry of the cross. Well does the Letter say, Jesus "offered" his prayers and supplications. For his cry is not an animal cry, an unconscious, biological reaction. The cry of Jesus is a call to the Father in the name of all of his persecuted children. It has almost a ritual value: it is part of Jesus' sacrifice and priestly ministry. Through Jesus on the cross, all the oppressed of the world "offer prayers and supplications with loud cries and tears to God, who is able to save them from death."

Jesus' cry confers dignity and rights on all of the poor, on all those deprived of their rights. Without this cry, what good would these rights be? Does not the law of the mightiest, the law of natural selection, triumph throughout the world of matter and living beings? Have not thousands of vegetable and animal species been eliminated in this struggle for life? Why would human beings, vanquished in the process of survival of the fittest, have more rights than animals bested in the same contest? Will not the greater vigor ever be the one to triumph?

Ancient civilizations always practiced the right of the mightiest. Even today, in wars, might makes right. To the victor, all rights; to the vanquished, suppression of those rights. This law is still accepted and acknowledged in our world today. A general who wins never goes to trial, and the basic reproach to the vanquished is not that they have committed crimes against life and justice—but that they have been defeated.

Then why these rights of the conquered? What is their basis? Something mightier than biological laws. Something mightier than the laws of nations, mightier than wars. The author of these rights is God—God who is so rarely recognized in practice by any of the mighty of the world.

Jesus sought to learn what it means to be human, sought to know the human condition of the vanquished of this world. And he experienced total defeat. Surely it is total defeat to be displayed to the eyes of the world nailed to a cross. Surely this is the supreme demonstration of weakness, to feel the weight of oppression, and domination, and the gaze of satisfaction and arrogance of the dominators—to serve as a plaything in the hands of one's enemies.

But more than anything else, Jesus sought solidarity with all men and women, and the right to represent them in this universal cry.

THE CRY OF JESUS AND FAITH

Jesus' cry is the expression of pain, deep physical pain in the struggle with death. It is not a fictitious cry. It is the shout of a body really being destroyed.

And yet, still more than an expression of bodily pain, this cry is an expression of faith. The Letter to the Hebrews explains the secret of the cross and the cry of Christ:

> Let us keep our eyes fixed on Jesus, who inspires and perfects our faith. For the sake of the joy which lay before him he endured the cross, heedless of its shame [Heb. 12:2].

Jesus lived his faith on the cross. On the cross, Jesus is creator, source, and fulfiller of faith. His cry was an act of faith. Of his own free will he took the road of the cross. Once the devil had beckoned him to the road of triumph, but he preferred the path of his oppressed brothers and sisters. And so he became one of them. He refused to accept complicity with the dominators.

Along the solid route of faith, Jesus persevered to the end, and this in the face of the greatest challenge of all: death.

What is faith? The Letter to the Hebrews, recalling many a case of faith in the Old Testament, gives us the best definition: To have faith is to make invisible things come to be. With faith, what was invisible becomes visible. Through faith, what is not seen is as real as what is seen. Faith makes what is not seen exist. By faith, what is not seen is treated as seriously as what is seen. You have faith when you build your life on something invisible.

There is nothing more invisible than the God of the poor and oppressed. It costs the conquerors and oppressors nothing to acknowledge their own gods. The advantages they receive are sufficient warranty for them of the power of their gods, just as for the conquered and oppressed it is as if their God had disappeared, and become invisible once more.

To have faith is to rest one's life continuously on God, even when, in defeat, God seems absent. To have faith is to build one's life continuously on God's promises, even though the visible fruits of these promises are so impalpable that all appears unreal. To have faith is to believe without seeing, as Jesus explained to Thomas in the Gospel of John.

Nailed to the cross, Jesus seemed alone, abandoned by the Father. And yet with his cry—with this act of faith—Jesus spoke to his Father, clinging to him, and calling to him when everything seemed gone.

To be right when victory is yours is easy. What is hard is to believe that you are right when the reality of the visible world contradicts you. How often it happens that the vanquished conclude from their defeat that they have been wrong—that right was not on their side but on that of the mightier. To resist this temptation then—to shout "No!"—is what it means to have faith.

Jesus' faith crowns the faith of the "ancients." The Letter to the Hebrews cites the most important cases. The history of faith began with Abel. It continued with Enoch, Noah, Abraham, Isaac, Jacob, Moses, and the ancients who entered the land of promise. Then came the Judges, David, the prophets, and all the righteous persecuted (Heb. 11). For them all, life was a constant struggle, amid failure, want, and persecution. But they stayed strong.

For them, God's invisible promises were reality—the true reality, for which they had sacrificed all. Of them all, it can be said what Hebrews says of the patriarchs:

> All of these died in faith. They did not obtain what had been promised but saw and saluted it from afar. By acknowledging themselves to be strangers and foreigners on the earth, they showed that they were seeking a homeland [Heb. 11:13].

It was Moses who best prefigured the faith of Jesus Christ:

> By faith Moses, when he had grown up, refused to be known as the son of Pharaoh's daughter; he wished to be ill-treated along with God's people rather than enjoy the fleeting rewards of sin. Moses considered the reproach borne by God's Anointed greater riches than the treasures of Egypt, for he was looking to the reward [Heb. 11:24–26].

Thus he emulated Jesus, who renounced the privileges of his perfection to adopt the condition of his sisters and brothers. The Letter to the Hebrews says of Moses:

> By faith he left Egypt, not fearing the king's wrath, for
> he persevered as if he were looking on the invisible God
> [Heb. 11:27].

Faith, then, is to keep one's eyes fixed on the invisible, as if
one were gazing upon the Invisible One itself.

All of these "ancients" were the forerunners of the faith of
Jesus, and of the cross, and Jesus recalls the example of each.
He knows that he is heir to the heroes of faith. He recalls the
struggles, the temptations, of all of these ancient ones who
opened the way for him. When he was dying on the cross,
Jesus saw himself in continuity with all who had believed
before him in the same circumstances. They believed in God
and clung to him, and just as they, Jesus, too, clung to his
Father and held tight to the promises.

Jesus' cry is the echo of the Psalms, as we have said. He
knows that all of the ancient heroes of faith raised the same
shout, and that the faith of them all was to culminate in his
own faith. And so his great cry is as the recapitulation of the
immense call of all Israel. Unfortunately, it is in a world that
believes in force, in power, in victory and domination, that
this cry, Israel's act of faith, is raised. Unfortunately, Israel's
leaders clung to the world, and to its false protests of loyalty.

Now, faith is not found in Israel alone. Among the pagans,
too, as we read, once more, in Hebrews, we find models of
faith. There is Abel. There is Enoch, and Noah. These represent the multitudes of true believers among the peoples of all
times. They all built their lives on the Invisible One, although
they gave that One various names. Outside Israel, too, many
were those who resisted temptations to power and domination along the path of Moses and Jesus. Many were those who
struggled without seeing the outcome of their struggles. With
their gaze fixed on the true God, they kept far from the idols
of might and domination. Out of the darkness they cried,
without knowing the name of the One they invoked.

In Jesus, who stands in continuity with all these brothers and sisters among far-flung peoples, from the Far East to the West, the faith of all men and women will at last be culminated. On the cross, he is the bearer of this tireless faith that has been struggling all these thousands of years.

Now, Jesus represents not only the .end of an ancient lineage, but the beginning of a new history, as well. On his act of faith will depend millions of others—those of his followers.

He gave his disciples the mission of imitating him—of following him, emulating him, living as he lives, acting as he acts, making the options that he makes. And what will be the key moment in this imitation? The cross. Of all the actions of Jesus, none will attract more eyes. All eyes are on the cross. As Zechariah proclaimed, and as John calls out in his Gospel: "They shall look on him whom they have pierced" (John 19:37; Zech. 12:10).

What is it that his disciples gaze on? Jesus' faith. They look and listen. They hear Jesus' cry, the call of faith in the Father. For Jesus' cry was to be a cry that "started something"—started the faith of the generations to come.

Jesus defeated fear and death by his faith. Death failed to destroy him or shake his faith. And so the disciples fixed their eyes on Jesus on the cross when they were assaulted by fear and the power of death. For them, Jesus' cry was a call and a summons to repeat the same cry.

Jesus' faith on the cross was the resurrection of a new people, the signal for the awakening of a faith that had gone to sleep, or gone out, in the hearts of human beings. And this cross of Jesus is the great sign, the great cry raised among the nations, the bond linking them all, past, present, and future.

After all, faith is not born of the ordinary processes of human training. It is transmitted from person to person. Faith is a chain, running back through peoples and generations. Formal instruction can spread the words of faith, but it cannot spread faith. The words are left empty, they collapse in indifference, when faith disappears. No, faith is born only of contact with other faith. And the first link in the chain is Jesus on the cross—Jesus emitting his cry—his culminating act of faith, before the Father, and before the world.

After two thousand years, the object of faith is as invisible as it was at the beginning. After all, faith consists in seeing the invisible. The object of our faith is like a pearl—so very small, but in order to buy it we must sell all that we have. It is like leaven—invisible in the dough. Jesus' experience on the cross is our experience still. The false illusions of Christendom have vanished, leaving us with nothing but the conviction we had from the start: that the kingdom of God is still a leaven in the dough.

THE CRY OF JESUS AND HOPE

The faith of the ancients was faith in the promises—pure hope, with little support in experience. The faith of Jesus on the cross, too, contains a hope. Only this time it is much more specific. This time it is hope in resurrection and eternal life. Jesus' cry is a call to the Father. It is also a cry of confidence in the resurrection. As the Letter to the Hebrews says, Jesus called to the One who could save him from death. His cry is a scream of trust in the resurrection.

Thus, in his death, Jesus lives the greatest of contradictions; he experiences the greatest of paradoxes: at the very moment that he surrenders his spirit in death, he proclaims victory over death.

Saint Luke expresses this aspect of Jesus' cry by placing on his lips the words, "Father, into your hands I commend my spirit" (Luke 23:46).

In Jesus the ancient cry becomes utterly new. The ancients cried out, and trusted, but did not know what the Father's response would be. With Jesus it is different. He knows that his own death is exactly the way that the Father had determined for death's defeat and the establishment of the reign of life. Jesus' death, as a sacrifice lived by him and offered to the Father, is the hidden means selected by the Father to ensure the triumph of life for human beings. Death is no longer the perfect vacuum separating the believer from the Father's promises. Death is now the path to resurrection.

Dying, surrendering his spirit—"expiring"—Jesus knows that he is fulfilling the act by which death is defeated. Jesus' death is an action, and an efficacious action. And so, at the moment of expiring, Jesus knows that he is winning—that he is defeating death. His confidence is total, because the act of his defeat is at the same time the act of victory over that which defeats him.

And so Saint John places on Jesus' lips, in the moment of his death, the words of a victory cry: "Now it is finished!" (John 19:30). Just before his arrest Jesus had told his disciples, "I have overcome the world" (John 16:33). Jesus' cry on the cross is a shout of victory.

The certainty of Jesus' resurrection actually transforms the tone of the Old Testament cry itself. With Jesus, the times have come when defeat is victory, suffering is delight, sorrow is gladness, death and life are lived simultaneously, in a complex experience. This experience outstrips all psychological categories and logical explanations. There is no rational connection between the two poles of death and life—only a superabundance of vitality in Christ and his followers.

From this moment forward we must maintain a balance between the two aspects of the cry. The cry of Jesus was surely a cry of pain and suffering. It was, and continues to be, the intense cry of an oppression that reigned, and reigns still, the length and breadth of humanity. It was the reaction of a being cut to the quick, slashed to the bone—the lamentation of one humiliated and reduced to helplessness.

The price of Jesus' victory was precisely his acceptance of suffering in the midst of failures and victories. Thanks to failure, victory was won, and death gave place to life.

At the same time, in spite of all appearances to the contrary, at the moment when Jesus hung on the cross the invisible victory of resurrection was present. It was a certainty, but an impalpable certainty, and therefore the object of faith. However near, resurrection never lost its character as object of hope.

To be sure, Jesus transformed the calls of the Old Testament, transformed them profoundly, in such wise that a rereading of the Bible with a starting point in Christ gives it a wholly new meaning and vigor. The light of the resurrection and of the coming of the kingdom of God bestowed a greater value on the faith of the ancients. No, they had not been crying out in vain. Now the cry that had been accumulating and swelling down the course of the centuries finds its final, most magnificent response.

Chapter Three

The Cry of the Sons and Daughters of God

The cry of the oppressed Israelite people has not lost its value in the time of the New Testament—the era in which we live.

After all, and first of all, just as Jesus focused all of the realities of the Old Testament in his cry, so also did these realities find in him their own complete realization. And so if we would understand Jesus better, we would do well to draw near the world of the Old Testament. Only here shall we grasp the full meaning of Jesus' cry at the moment of dying. There is no other way to seize the sense of this cry than to gather up the recollection of the cry of God's people down through the Old Testament, all through the history of Israel. Jesus' annihilation and humiliation gain their human scope and depth in light of the experiences, the oppressions, of the people of Israel, which are a matter of historical record thanks to the Old Testament, which narrates these events and confers on them their meaning. The faith-value with which Christ's cry is laden would vanish like smoke were it not for the testimony of faith of the sons and daughters of Israel, who selected the cry as the way to express their dignity and their unshakable trust in God, who is the foundation and warranty of the dignity of the members of the chosen people.

Second, the value of the Old Testament stands intact because, since Jesus Christ, the historical existence of peoples continues. It did not reach its fulfillment with the death and resurrection of Christ. That was only the beginning of the end, the victory that guarantees the future, the seed of the kingdom of God. Neither the oppression nor the humiliation of the poor came to an end. And the coming of Christ projects upon this oppression and humiliation a new light, which intensifies faith.

The history of ancient Israel, then, stands before us as a paradigm—as the great explanatory sign of the history of God's new people, formed from among the peoples of the earth starting with Israel. And the destiny of the new people of God will have its explanation and model in Israel. This new people will be able to find in the Bible the meaning of events, and not have to suffer oppression as an inevitable cataclysm, or humiliation as a sign of moral inferiority. This new people will be able to enjoy the dignity of daughters and sons of God, for they will be able to count on the help and advocacy of the Father in times of extreme need.

We have meditated on the cry of the people of Israel and its culmination in the cry of Jesus. Let us now examine, in the texts of the New Testament, the lot of God's new people. We shall be able to grasp the meaning of their cry in Jesus, in the church, and in a world renewed by Jesus' death and resurrection.

CRY OF THE MARTYRS

In New Testament times the first echo of Israel's cry is in the voice of the martyrs. In the theology of Christian martyrdom, the martyrs continue the role of the prophets and the other persons in the Old Testament who were just and who were victims of persecution. The martyrs are the incarnation of God's new people, the new Israel, which passes through the same historical phases as the ancient people.

It is in the Book of Revelation that the theology of martyrdom is best developed in the Bible. This last book of the Bible projects a vision of the new Israel in its history to come. It does not furnish a view of future events in their particularity and contingency. It offers us a vision of the meaning and the value that will attach to these future events.

The Christian martyrs bring something new to the meaning of the people of Israel. This new element places the martyrs more in the line of the prophets than in that of the people of Israel as a whole. The people of Israel as a whole were oppressed and persecuted without deliberate cause on their part. They were a conquered people, and like any conquered people they were subjugated by the conquering people. They were victims of the law of war—the law of natural selection as applied to peoples. But with the martyrs—as with the prophets—things were different. The martyrs were oppressed because of their own acts. They had proclaimed the gospel of Christ, and defied the established idols—whether in the form of religious authorities or in the form of political ones. Their acts were a provocation, and aroused repression—which is the form oppression takes in cases like theirs.

Like the people of Israel, the martyrs have the right to cry out to Yahweh, to protest the treatment they receive. For theirs is the dignity of the people of God. There is a covenant between them and God, and that covenant stipulates their right to call on God for help.

Like the prophets, their forerunners, the martyrs have more right to this appeal than the oppressed people in Egypt. They are persecuted, oppressed, tortured, and killed precisely because they have toiled for God's cause. What has provoked their oppression has not been activity undertaken on their own initiative—crimes they have decided to commit "on their own." No, they are persecuted for obeying God's orders, for acting in the name of Christ, who, in turn, has sent them forth in his Father's name. It is scarcely too much to ask that God take up their defense, when it is their service to God that has occasioned such perils. They have brought death upon themselves by carrying out the orders of Christ in the name of the Father.

Perhaps we may better understand all this by looking at the persecution suffered by the new people of Christ. For here the persecuted are Christ himself and God his Father. The adversaries think that they have silenced and annihilated this people by exterminating its witnesses. The martyrs are not attacked for what they are, or for anything they do on their own account. They are attacked to destroy God's kingdom. In raising their cry, the martyrs ask only that God defend himself—his honor, his kingdom, and his glory.

The Book of Revelation shows us two versions of the martyrs' cry. It takes two different points of view. This book, as we know, represents Christian subjects visually. It is a book of visions, and each vision illustrates an aspect of revelation. The visions are complementary, however, and have Christian value only in their complementarity. Each vision considered separately looks like a text of pure Jewish "apocalyptic." It is their juxtaposition that produces the Christian effect.

The cry of the martyrs, then, had to have its two antithetical aspects. Now that Christ had come, everything had changed. No longer was the cry of a martyr purely and simply a cry of death. It was a shout of victory, too. In the Book of Revelation, these two aspects of their cry are presented as two different cries, in two different visions.

The first vision is in chapter 6. It shows the martyrs in the form of blood flowing over the altar. The visionary sees the martyrs' "spirits," that is, their lives, flowing down to the foot of the altar in the form of blood, like the blood of the victims slain by the priest in Jewish sacrifices. And the "spirits" of these martyrs call out to God:

> I saw under the altar the spirits of those who had been martyred because of the witness they bore to the word of God. They cried out at the top of their voices: "How long will it be, O Master, holy and true, before you judge our cause and avenge our blood among the inhabitants of the earth?" [Rev. 6:9–10].

As with the death of Christ, the death of the martyrs has sacrificial value. It is linked to the sacrifice of Christ. It is the continuation, the living presence, of the sacrifice of Christ in his members. It wins salvation.

Here the martyrs are manifesting pure oppression. The blood they shed speaks, and demands justice. But they lie in defeat at the foot of the altar. Now, in the presence of God, their blood enters into God's plans. It flows in the place where decisions are made as to the world's fate. The cry is there for good and for all. It has been gathered up by God and abides in God's presence. And the world's fate is tied to this cry. God responds to it by the decisions God makes concerning the world's future.

What the sacred writer seeks to show us here is not simply that the martyrs suffer, crying out in the midst of their torture—but that their plaint is the spring that moves the world, that God's justice is in motion to answer the martyrs' cry.

The purpose of the sacred writer in recounting this vision is to encourage the martyrs—to show them the great power of their cry. The justice of God will be effective and implacable, for the martyrs have cried for justice, and the martyrs have great power before God.

The second vision is in chapter 7. The martyrs return, but this time the story is very different. This time they form a great multitude, like a huge, peaceful army, wearing their medals of victory. And this time their cry is a victory shout, the cry of a conquering army acclaiming its leader:

> They stood before the throne and the Lamb, dressed in long white robes and holding palm branches in their hands. They cried out in a loud voice, "Salvation is from our God, who is seated on the throne, and from the Lamb!" [Rev. 7:9–10].

They are the martyrs:

> These are the ones who have survived the great period of trial; they have washed their robes and made them white in the blood of the Lamb [Rev. 7:14].

They have shared in the tribulation of Christ's death. They have passed the test. They have survived the trial of the Lamb.

Now the martyrs are conquerors. They can foresee their resurrection. For the vision in chapter 7 is a vision of the future, a vision of the New Jerusalem. The martyrs of today are on the road to the New Jerusalem of tomorrow. They already share in the pledges of the coming reign of God. They walk in the company of the risen Christ. Their cry is as the cry of triumph of Christ on the cross. It is a cry of light and victory.

Thus the martyrs, visibly suffering the worst humiliation and abandonment at the hands of their torturers, share beforehand, by faith, the resurrection of Jesus, the resurrection of the cross. The resurrection will not come later, as an act of justice, as God's response to the martyrs' calls. It is already present. Already, at this very moment, the martyrs can raise their voices in tones of triumph, because eternal life is theirs right now—in the very moment of their struggle with their murderers. They have already attained immortality, and death does them harm only on the surface of their being. They are conquerors—the true conquerors—in the very moment of their visible defeat. And they are themselves convinced that they share in the resurrection and death of Jesus. In death itself they live the resurrection.

The first testimony to Christian martyrdom is found in the Acts of the Apostles. It reports the martyrdom of Saint Stephen. As the first martyr, Stephen could not refrain from imitating Christ and renewing, resuming, the ancient cry of Israel in Egypt. He too cried out with a loud voice, like the cry of the people in the old history of the time of the Judges, or like the cry of the Psalms. The cry of Jesus lived once more in the cry of Stephen.

The "Acts" of the martyrs reflect the very same theology of martydom as does the Book of Revelation. And, indeed, Stephen lived martyrdom in the same way as those that Saint John describes in chapter 7 of the Book of Revelation. Stephen lived his martyrdom like a conqueror. He died, but he won the battle. In chapter 7 of Acts, Luke writes of Stephen's martyrdom:

> Stephen meanwhile, filled with the Holy Spirit, looked to the sky above and saw the glory of God, and Jesus standing at God's right hand. "Look!" he exclaimed, "I see an opening in the sky, and the Son of Man standing at God's right hand" [Acts 7:55–56].

Jesus appears to Stephen as a judge, on his feet, and ready to stride forth—like someone on his way, like someone about to judge the universe and restore justice. Stephen's martyrdom only hastens the Last Judgment. Jesus is coming to avenge his prophets, and among them his faithful martyr Stephen, who contemplates Christ's victory and proclaims it.

Before he dies, Stephen repeats Jesus' last cry as we have read it in the Gospel of Luke: "Lord Jesus," he calls, "receive my spirit" (Acts 7:59; see Luke 23:46). And then he says—once more in Jesus' words—"Lord, do not hold this sin against them" (Acts 7:60; see Luke 23:24). And the writer of Acts, who is also the writer of Luke, recalls that Stephen "cried out in a loud voice" (Acts 7:60), as Jesus had, before dying—cried out with the shout that resounds, since the days of Abel, from the throats of the oppressed of the whole universe, as they cry out for divine liberation.

According to the Book of Revelation, the martyrs represent the whole church. After all, the whole church, the totality of the people of God, finds itself in a state of persecution, and bears witness before the powers of the world. The church is a challenge to the world and its authorities. Thus it brings on itself all opposition to the truth, all the forces of death and the lie. Not all die literally, and not all suffer at the same hour. But because the whole church lives in an ongoing state of martyrdom, under sentence of death at the heart of the world, the martyrs are its most meaningful representatives.

This being the case, the cry of the martyrs is, we might say, a permanent one. It is an ongoing office in the people of God. Nor does the church live its martyrdom at a determinate hour. The church is like a martyrdom extending over the earth and embracing it continuously. The cry, then, is part and parcel of the church's manner of being.

The church is a voice rising to God and crying for justice to the poor and oppressed. It is the voice of the marginalized, who can no longer express themselves, and feel so powerless and helpless.

Through the liturgy, the celebration of the word, the church utters its denunciation, for all ears to hear, of the injustice being committed against the poor and oppressed, the people of God. And it is just because the church is the martyr's cry—just because it takes this role upon itself—that it must be persecuted, and be the continuous witness of these martyrs.

THE CRY OF THE SONS AND DAUGHTERS OF GOD

We come now to the passages that present the cry of the poor most explicitly. The cry of the martyrs, being the cry of Christ on the cross taken up and cried once more by the church, is the most meaningful expression of the cry of God's people. But it is not the only cry of God's people. It is not even their more usual cry. Christ himself lived the cry of God's people before pronouncing it in its ultimate form, on the cross.

The passages from Saint Paul that we are about to cite form the crowning point in the development of a theme that runs throughout the whole Bible. In retrospect, these passages afford us a better understanding of everything that has gone before. The point of destination sheds light on all of the points along the way.

These passages are key indeed—the crowning point of all of the novelty of the gospel. They show us the central focus of Christ's fulfillment in the Holy Spirit. They are the faithful summary of what is new in the gospel:

The proof that you are sons is the fact that God has sent forth into our hearts the spirit of his Son which cries out "Abba!" ("Father!") [Gal. 4:6].

All who are led by the Spirit of God are sons of God. You did not receive a spirit of slavery leading you back into fear, but a spirit of adoption through which we cry out, "Abba!" (that is, "Father") [Rom. 8:14–15].

This cry is the exclusive privilege of sons and daughters. By the cry, a person is recognizable as a child of God. Not everyone can address the Father with confidence. For not everyone has access to him, only those selected by the Father himself to be his daughters and sons.

These know that the Father is committed to them. They know that between the Father and themselves is a solidarity that nothing can breach. And so they refuse to bow their heads to an almighty fatalism, after the manner of slaves.

Our contemporaries, reared in an age of science and reason, are no longer able to call to a Father. For them the world follows only rigid laws of necessity. The world, and all human beings, must accept the determinisms of necessity. The age of fear has returned. It is of no avail to ask and supplicate in the hour of need. No prayer, in their mind, can influence the course of events, the evolution of nature and society. There is no longer any Father who might be able to come to their aid. Everything is determined beforehand, subject to the material forces present in the world and observed by science. For them, the cry has lost its meaning.

Or at least so it seems. In reality, they are homesick for their lost Father. And they continue to raise their voices in indignation at the oppression all about them, as if there were someone to witness it. They appeal to history, as if there were someone capable of hearing history. They pass judgment, as if there were rules that could confer any meaning on their judgments. They cannot accustom themselves to an empty universe—empty of presences, eyes, ears, sensibilities, and emotions.

Thus reason is becoming progressively rationalistic, evacuating the world of the presences with which it had been peopled, leaving only quantitative relations, among mutually relative terms. And yet, at the same time, subjective sensibilities accept any new religion that offers new presences—for no better reason than that people are hungry for them, and that this hunger needs calming. All around us new religions are springing up, heirs of more ancient ones, animisms, polytheisms, and oriental gnoses. All of these presences seek to replace the forgotten Father. They all seem to believe that human beings can create for themselves, to their image and likeness, powerful gods to satisfy their anxieties.

Now, actually, there is a Father. And this Father is not the work of human hands. No one has access to the Father unless he or she has been called and has responded by total faith and a radical change of life.

There is a Father. But he cannot be manipulated, functioning only if someone has need of him. The Father chooses his daughters and sons. No one can be a son or daughter of God unless he or she is adopted by God.

The privilege of being a son or daughter of God can be truly understood only within the biblical perspective of God's "seriousness." The new, modern religions claiming to be inspired in the East, and so like the ancient gnoses of primitive Christian times, propose divinities that lack "seriousness." These forces, or spirits, supposedly superior gods or beings, are really but the figment of human vanity, and naturally lend themselves to all the fantasies of those who claim to venerate them, while really but using them for their own self-satisfaction. Their devotees call themselves the "children" of these divinities. Then they are the children of nothing at all, because these divinities are nothing but the projection of human subjectivity.

The God of the Bible is the only God there is. Therefore he is inaccessible. As Saint Thomas said, the only way to speak correctly of God is in negative fashion. We can tell all that God is *not*, but not what God *is*. For God is beyond all of our ideas and conceptualizations. Saint John said it most arrestingly: Never has anyone seen God. Never has anyone had direct knowledge of God. None of our words, of themselves, can say anything about God.

It is a profound and incomprehensible mystery that this God, while totally different from us, allows us to give him the name of Father, allows this word to have a certain content in his regard. Make no mistake, to be a son or daughter of this God is strictly contingent on God's sovereign choice. Who could even imagine the least condition imposed on the true God, God who is beyond the universe—not only as the one giving life to that universe, but as infinitely superior to it? An appreciation of the title of "children of God" is contingent on a proper appreciation of God's transcendence—of the radical distance separating God from any conceptualization we may have of him. And yet Saint Paul declares that we can approach this God—that we have access to him as his daughters and sons.

When Paul writes "us," of whom is he speaking? He does not mean the whole of humanity. And yet neither is he speaking of any particular individual. By "we" and "us" he means the true Israel, the people of God, risen and sprung from Jesus Christ as the "true remnant" of God's chosen people. From this true remnant, heir to ancient Israel—first Jesus alone, on the cross, then we—a new Israel is born, an Israel that has dropped all pretensions, an Israel made of all those poor who have abandoned every desire and prop of the human power of culture and civilization to live a faith in Christ, identifying with him and laboring in his service. Those who have been baptized in Jesus' death and resurrection have left behind all ambitions of this world, and have entered upon a new life of service in the following of Jesus. These are the true sons and daughters of God, assimilated to the one true Son, and they are sons and daughters of God because they are identified with his son Jesus Christ.

The sons and daughters of God are moved by the very Spirit of God, so that now their own spirits no longer move on their own initiative alone, but it is the Spirit of God who gives them their energy—a new energy, with a new scope. Only the Spirit of God can stream into a person's heart and emit the cry, "Father!"

Of course, this name seems to us to be so easy to pronounce that at times we judge God's intervention unnecessary. It is such a simple operation, we feel. But it is not a matter of simply pronouncing a word. If the privilege of crying, "Father!" were the simple matter of the pronunciation of a word, it would be hard to see why the Spirit would be necessary. Nor would it be easy to see why the privilege of daughter or son is so great.

But it is not a matter of pronouncing a word, as one recites a prayer. It is not a matter of formality. What Saint Paul offers Christians is the opportunity to relive Jesus' experience on the cross. On the cross Jesus was able to concentrate, in his voice alone, the cry of the whole of humanity, and the cry of the poor of all times. Jesus was able to express all of the world's pain, all of its pleading for justice and liberation. In his humiliation Jesus lived the abasement of all the conquered and oppressed. On the cross, Jesus experienced the disaster of so many human lives implacably eliminated by the march of history's conquerors. He offered "prayers and supplications," with "loud cries and tears." He expressed the call that the people, the poor, have a right to express, with a faith that nothing could shake, as if he were gazing upon the Invisible One. He expressed an infallible hope, and this hope has sunk its roots deep in the hearts of the poor of the earth.

And we are called to make the same prayer—to pray once more the prayer of Jesus on the cross. We too can gather up, on our daily cross, all of the suffering of the oppressed of the world—in our persecution, the persecution of all the just, living, in all its extension, the cry of the poor, and transforming the cry of pain into a cry of hope and faith. And extending Jesus' victory over fear and death to our very day, we can live the freedom of Jesus on the cross and, by our faith, conquer.

The Spirit of God, who is also the Spirit of Jesus Christ, opens up our own spirits to be able to take on ourselves the whole history of pain, struggle, and faith. The Spirit enables us to emerge from the narrow limits of the events of our personal lives to accomplish a fusion between our crucifixion and the crucifixion of the world, between our resurrection and the resurrection of the world: to be the channels by which Christ extends his cry to all of the oppressed in all generations—and, concretely, to the oppressed of our generation, and of the historical place to which we have been sent.

Only the Spirit of Christ could ever have awakened in us that experience of life that reproduces in us the experience of Jesus on the cross. Without the Spirit, perhaps indeed we could reproduce something of the cry of the Israelite people in Egypt—but never, surely, the cry of Jesus on the cross. Even the cry of Israel in Egypt had something of the Spirit about it. Without the Spirit, the poor could groan, and utter their plaint—but not make of their abasement a victory of faith through hope, nor conquer slavery and live in freedom even while nailed to a cross. But the "Abba, Father!" that Jesus has taught us means all of this. For it was the Spirit who taught Jesus this same cry, on the cross.

The Spirit of God places us above the entire world, high on the cross, from whose pinnacle we perceive humanity as Jesus perceived it. We hear the cry of all the oppressed. We behold a compendium of history from Abel's time onward. We contemplate what the systems of civilizations conceal. We unmask the lies of the false prophets who claim that peace, order, and tranquillity are already here, that we are well off, that "all is well"—that we are making progress, that everything is being taken care of. This is the lie arranged by the dominators and their public relations machines and their media. But we see the history of men and women from the vantage of the victims, as Jesus saw it on the cross, and felt it in his own flesh. He saw and felt the *reality* of this world. And so do we.

Now, it was from this vantage that Jesus saw and heard

that Yahweh, the Father, was the Father of these oppressed, these victims. He had faith, and withdrew from the false images of the idols who always agree with the oppressors. He understood that God was committed, once for all, to the cause of the oppressed.

The cry of Christians, then, is the expression of the cry of the world's oppressed, extending the cry of Jesus to the world's length and breadth, and helping this cry embrace the world from generation to generation. The voice of Christians prolongs and extends the voice of Christ, breaking the world's silence about its terrible reality, overcoming and vanquishing fear. Christians, in their turn, no longer allow themselves to be led by the false prudence of fear, but dare to burst the barrier of silence and complicity with sin. No longer are they borne along by the spirit of fear; no longer are they slaves of fear. Knowing that they are sons and daughters of God, because they have achieved their liberty, they can raise their voice. They can look resistance and repression in the face, for the Father is with them, and will defend them in the hour of witness and martyrdom.

And yet, like the cry of Jesus on the cross, the cry of Christians is an act of faith. It is the triumph of faith over historical appearances. It is a cry of victory when defeat is so obvious! At the very moment when they are as nothing before the world, Jesus' followers approach the Father and show him their faith. Faith is confidence in triumph despite all appearances, despite everything visible. It is the Spirit who makes this act of faith possible. God's power may appear hidden. Sin and injustice may appear to dominate the world, smashing all the forces of change. But despite everything, God's sons and daughters persevere. They do not lose heart. They assert their faith. They trust in the power of their Father, crying out to him in the certitude that he will liberate his abased people.

In the church, then, the act of faith is the continuing

presence of Jesus' act of faith on the cross. There Jesus placed his trust in the Father, and looked to the future at the very moment when all seemed in the depths of despair. So did his disciples. After all, faith is not the expression of an awareness of what is present. Faith is the expression not of what is seen, but of what is not seen. This cry truly shows how to live the faith, and Christians live the faith from a situation of oppression, from the heights of the cross, the moment the Spirit becomes present to rid them of all the deficiencies of their perceptions, revealing to them the invisible, and inspiring in them trust in the absent.

When Christians utter their cry, they point to the resurrection of Jesus. For this is the sign of the promise. Nor was this promise made in vain, for Jesus' resurrection was itself an act of faith. All of this is wrapped in faith—in a faith that proclaims that God's triumph is already begun, that the shout of victory has already resounded. We call on the Father relying on the fact of the resurrection, so that our cry is also thanksgiving for what the Father has already done.

Yes, the cry is hope in the final resurrection, hope in the future. It begins with the beginning of resurrection in Jesus. Jesus' cry has already reached the kingdom of God, and abides at the right hand of the Father. It is the cry that organizes world history and gives it direction. Christians know that this history is organized in function of themselves. Henceforward everything is to serve the spread of the gospel and the triumph of Christ, and there is nothing that can keep us from the Lord's victory.

Saint Paul himself comments on the cry of the Spirit at the conclusion of his disquisition on the mystery of liberation:

What shall we say after that? If God is for us, who can be against us? . . . Who shall bring a charge against God's chosen ones? God, who justifies? Who shall condemn them? Christ Jesus, who died or rather was raised up, who is at the right hand of God and who intercedes for us? [Rom. 8:31–34].

This is the victory of the oppressed:

Who will separate us from the love of Christ? Trial, or distress, or persecution, or hunger, or nakedness, or danger, or the sword? As Scripture says: "For your sake we are being slain all the day long; we are looked upon as sheep to be slaughtered." Yet in all this we are more than conquerors because of him who has loved us. For I am certain that neither death nor life, neither angels nor principalities, neither the present nor the future, nor powers, neither height nor depth nor any other creatures, will be able to separate us from the love of God that comes to us in Christ Jesus, our Lord [Rom. 8:35–39].

There could be no better commentary on the cry to the Father. On the one hand, the church of the poor and oppressed hears, repeats, and transmits the cry of the whole of creation:

Yes, we know that all creation groans and is in agony even until now [Rom. 8:22].

And:

Indeed, the whole created world eagerly awaits the revelation of the sons of God [Rom. 8:19].

By the Spirit, the disciples of Christ take up and express this same groaning. They too suffer, and in their suffering they look forward to the day of their liberation:

Not only that, but we ourselves, although we have the
Spirit as first fruits, groan inwardly while we await the
redemption of our bodies [Rom. 8:23].

On the other hand, this groaning is transformed into a
victory shout, for the Father has already begun his deed of
liberation, and we are victors in the very midst of oppression.

Looking back over the whole development of the cry of the
poor, from its very beginnings, we observe a slow matura-
tion. As Paul says: even before the slavery of Egypt, slavery
and oppression reigned in the world, and this oppression
affected not only the people of Israel, but all creation. True,
at first the cry was more like a groan than a call. God's name
was unknown. On whom could one call? With Moses, with
Israel in Egypt, God began to manifest himself, striking a
covenant with his people. From that moment forward, Israel
could point to that covenant. Now the cry was no longer a
groan, but a call.

God heard Israel's cry because it had actually been inspired by God's Spirit. It had come forth from God, and to
God it must return. The Israelites, on their way to adoption
by God, could already cry out as God's children. Through the
cry of Israel God was preparing the cry of his own Son on the
cross—the cry that would be repeated from that moment
onward by so many millions of voices, in every quarter of the
earth. Rightly could Jesus gather up the whole cry of Israel.
For that cry had indeed been the forerunner of the cry on the
cross.

CONTINUATION OF THE OLD TESTAMENT

The cry of an oppressed Israel culminates in the cry of
Christ and of the church. Nor are these two disconnected
cries. Both embrace their analogous Old Testament cries. For
oppression only culminates in the cross. It does not terminate

there. It continues, in the voice of the oppressed who cry to the Father, joining their cry to the cry of Jesus and of his whole body.

Saint James gives us an example of this cry of the oppressed poor as it continues today—more today than ever because it has awakened consciences:

> As for you, you rich, weep and wail over your impending miseries. . . . Here, crying aloud, are the wages you withheld from the farmhands who harvested your fields. The cries of the harvesters have reached the ears of the Lord of hosts [James 5:1–4].

The Letter of James recalls the realism of the gospel. Oppression is characterized most concretely in the form of harvesters who have not been paid the wages due them. Surely this is an almost trivial matter. Does this not happen every day? And millions of times a day? The cry of Jesus and the church springs up from the midst of a gigantic oppression, of which Israel's oppression was but an insignificant part. How much more has occurred since then! And yet, little by little, the harvesters of the fields of others have learned to raise their voice, to have confidence, to overcome their fear, and to denounce the lies by which they have been kept in servitude and silence.

The cry has not been without response. God replies. For the rights of the oppressed are the rights of God. Those who call on God and Jesus Christ may not remain indifferent to God's rights. They must take up their defense. The cry must effectuate a general mobilization of consciences, for the cry of the wronged poor is sacred. For all Christians, it comes first in importance and urgency.

The cry of the church, of which Saint Paul speaks, and the cry of the harvesters in James, are but one cry. Each receives its value and meaning from the other. They form the twin poles of a single cry. The harvesters' cry has value because it is carried by Jesus to the Father and taken up by Christ's church. And Jesus' cry becomes concretized in every age because it is the recapitulation of the cry of the harvesters and of all of the other exploited, deceived laborers over the face of the earth.

The Father's response is in the very cry, with its power in history. In taking up this cry, the church, and the whole Christian people, make it a factor in history.

Throughout Latin America, the church has been the mouthpiece of the oppressed more visibly today than in the past. Overcoming its fear, as Jesus overcame his, it has come forward in solidarity with the oppressed, the poor, and the marginalized. To use an expression that has become popular today, it has become "the voice of the voiceless."

The defense of human rights is today's cry of the people of God. Among the most sacred of human rights is the right of laborers to defend their own rights, and to be treated as persons, with dignity, both at work and in society. When this right is not respected, the supreme, ultimate right is the right to cry out. Jesus Christ claimed this right, and the church claims it in the name of oppressed workers. Thus does the church continue the ministry of Christ on earth.

The voice of the church bestows on the workers' cause a certain weight in history. And if this voice were to be raised more strongly still, this weight would be a good deal greater. The church, God's people, is a sign, and it acts by means of its own laborers, who take the initiative in arousing their sisters and brothers even when the church as an institution is not acting. And when the church as institution joins in—then the power of its witness increases, and the cry truly resounds, and has a great effect on history!

In no way may the church, as a human organization, be allowed to make use of the cry of the oppressed to promote its own expansion. However the church might, at times, serve political movements, or demagogues, or governments, as a tool of infiltration to neutralize the cry of the poor—this is an act of treachery to its divine calling. If priests so wished, for example, they might use the cry of the poor to cultivate the church's prestige among the poor, thus placing the voice of the Holy Spirit at the service of private interests.

Between the cry of the poor and the church the same relation obtains as between the people of God and the church—between the church as God's people and the church as authority. The word of the church is at the service of the cry, "Abba, Father!" and not the other way around. This cry, "Abba, Father!" is the cry uttered today by the oppressed people of God—by the unemployed, by a people who must live on an income barely sufficient—at best—for the necessities of life, by a people who receive no justice because there is no one to defend their cause. And therefore, as Saint James says—they cry out. And this cry is the very cry of Jesus on the cross, still echoing in our own day.

Appendix

SCRIPTURE PASSAGES ON THE CRY
OF THE PAST

GENESIS 21:14-19

Early the next morning Abraham got some bread and a skin of water and gave them to Hagar. Then, placing the child on her back, he sent her away. As she roamed aimlessly in the wilderness of Beer-sheba, the water in the skin was used up. So she put the child down under a shrub, and then went and sat down opposite him, about a bowshot away; for she said to herself, "Let me not watch the child die." As she sat opposite him, he began to cry. God heard the boy's cry, and God's messenger called to Hagar from heaven: "What is the matter, Hagar? Don't be afraid; God has heard the boy's cry in this plight of his. Arise, lift up the boy and hold him by the hand; for I will make of him a great nation." Then God opened her eyes, and she saw a well of water. She went and filled the skin with water, and then let the boy drink.

EXODUS 3:7-12

But the LORD said, "I have witnessed the affliction of my people in Egypt and have heard their cry of complaint against their slave drivers, so I know well what they are suffering. Therefore I have come down to rescue them from the hands of the Egyptians and lead them out of that land into a good and spacious land, a land flowing with milk and honey, the country of the Canaanites, Hittites, Amorites, Perizzites, Hivites and Jebusites. So indeed the cry of the Israelites has reached me, and I have truly noted that the Egyptians are oppressing them. Come now! I will send you to Pharaoh to lead my people, the Israelites, out of Egypt."

But Moses said to God, "Who am I that I should go to Pharaoh and lead the Israelites out of Egypt?" He answered, "I will be with you."

EXODUS 6:5-7

And now that I have heard the groaning of the Israelites, whom the Egyptians are treating as slaves, I am mindful of my covenant. Therefore, say to the Israelites: I am the LORD. I will free you from the forced labor of the Egyptians and will deliver you from their slavery. I will rescue you by my outstretched arm and with mighty acts of judgment. I will take you as my own people, and you shall have me as your God.

NUMBERS 20:16

When we cried to the LORD, he heard our cry and sent an angel [Moses] who led us out of Egypt.

DEUTERONOMY 26:6-9

When the Egyptians maltreated and oppressed us, imposing hard labor upon us, we cried to the LORD, the God of our fathers, and he heard our cry and saw our affliction, our toil and our oppression. He brought us out of Egypt with his strong hand and outstretched arm, with terrifying power, with signs and wonders; and bringing us into this country, he gave us this land flowing with milk and honey.

JUDGES 3:15-21

But when the Israelites cried out to the LORD, he raised up for them a savior, the Benjaminite Ehud, son of Gera, who was left-handed. It was by him that the Israelites sent their tribute to Eglon, king of Moab. Ehud made himself a two-edged dagger a foot long, and wore it under his clothes over his right thigh. He presented the tribute to Eglon, king of Moab, who was very fat, and after the presentation went off with the tribute bearers. He returned, however, from where the idols are, near Gilgal, and said, "I have a private message for you, O king." And the king said, "Silence!" Then when all his attendants had left his presence, and Ehud went in to him where he sat alone in his cool upper room, Ehud said, "I have a message from God for you." So the king rose from his chair, and then Ehud with his left hand drew the dagger from his right thigh, and thrust into Eglon's belly.

JUDGES 4:3-15; 5:1-31

[4] The Israelites cried out to the LORD. . . . At this time the prophetess Deborah, wife of Lappidoth, was judging Israel. She used to sit under Deborah's palm tree, situated between Ramah and Bethel in the mountain region of Ephraim, and there the Israelites came up to her for judgment. She sent and summoned Barak, son of Abinoam, from Kedesh of Naphtali. "This is what the LORD, the God of

Israel, commands," she said to him; "go, march on Mount
Tabor. . . ." Deborah also went up with him. . . .

So Sisera [the general of the enemy's army] assembled from
Harosheth-ha-goiim at the Wadi Kishon all nine hundred of
his iron chariots and all his forces. Deborah then said to
Barak, "Be off, for this is the day on which the LORD has
delivered Sisera into your power. The LORD marches before
you." So Barak went down Mount Tabor, followed by his ten
thousand men. And the LORD put Sisera and all his chariots
and all his forces to rout before Barak. . . .

[5] On that day Deborah sang this song: . . .

> In the days of Shamgar, son of Anath,
>   in the days of slavery caravans ceased;
> Those who traveled the roads
>   went by roundabout paths.
> Gone was freedom beyond the walls,
>   gone indeed from Israel.
> When I, Deborah, rose,
>   when I rose, a mother in Israel,
> New gods were their choice;
>   then the war was at their gates.
> Not a shield could be seen, nor a lance,
>   among forty thousand in Israel! . . .
>
> Awake, awake, Deborah!
>   awake, awake, strike up a song.
> Strength! arise, Barak,
>   make despoilers your spoil, son of Abinoam.
> Then down came the fugitives with the mighty,
>   the people of the LORD came down for me as
>   warriors. . . .

And the land was at rest for forty years.

JUDGES 10:11-16

The LORD answered the Israelites: "Did not the Egyptians, the Amorites, the Ammonites, the Philistines, the Sidonians, the Amalekites, and the Midianites oppress you? Yet when you cried out to me, and I saved you from their grasp, you still forsook me and worshiped other gods. Therefore I will save you no more. Go and cry out to the gods you have chosen; let them save you now that you are in distress." But the Israelites said to the LORD, "We have sinned. Do to us whatever you please. Only save us this day." And they cast out the foreign gods from their midst and served the LORD, so that he grieved over the misery of Israel.

JUDITH 7:19-29; 8:1-33; 9:1-14; 15:14; 16:17

[7]The Israelites cried to the LORD, their God, for they were disheartened, since all their enemies had them surrounded, and there was no way of slipping through their lines. The whole Assyrian camp, infantry, chariots, and cavalry, kept them thus surrounded for thirty-four days. All the reservoirs of water failed the inhabitants of Bethulia, and the cisterns ran dry, so that on no day did they have enough to drink, but their drinking water was rationed. Their children fainted away, and the women and youths were consumed with thirst and were collapsing in the streets and gateways of the city, with no strength left in them.

All the people, therefore, including youths, women, and children, went in a crowd to Uzziah and the rulers of the city. They set up a great clamor and said before the elders: "God judge between you and us! You have done us grave injustice in not making peace with the Assyrians. There is no help for us now! Instead, God has sold us into their power by laying us prostrate before them in thirst and utter exhaustion. Therefore, summon them and deliver the whole city as booty to the troops of Holofernes and to all his forces; we would be better off to become their prey. We should indeed be made slaves, but at least we should live, and not have to behold our little ones dying before our eyes and our wives and children breathing out their souls. We adjure you by heaven and earth, and by our God, the LORD of our forefathers, who is punishing us for our sins and those of our forefathers, to do as we have proposed, this very day."

All in the assembly with one accord broke into shrill wailing and loud cries to the LORD their god. . . .

[8] Now in those days Judith, daughter of Merari, . . . heard of this. . . . When Judith, therefore, heard of the harsh words which the people, discouraged by their lack of water, had spoken against their ruler, and of all that Uzziah had said to them in reply, swearing, that he would hand over the city to the Assyrians at the end of five days, she sent the maid who was in charge of all her things to ask Uzziah, Chabris, and Charmis, the elders of the city, to visit her. When they came, she said to them: "Listen to me, you rulers of the people of Bethulia. What you said to the people today is not proper. When you promised to hand over the city to our enemies at the end of five days unless within that time the LORD comes to our aid, you interposed between God and yourselves this oath which you took. Who are you, then, that you should have put God to the test this day, setting yourselves in the place of God in human affairs? It is the LORD Almighty for whom you are laying down conditions; will you never understand anything? You cannot plumb the depths of the human heart or grasp the workings of the human mind; how then can you fathom God, who has made all these things, discern his mind, and understand his plan? . . . So while we wait for the salvation that comes from him, let us

call upon him to help us, and he will hear our cry if it is his good pleasure." . . .

Then Judith said to them: "Listen to me! I will do something that will go down from generation to generation among the descendants of our race. Stand at the gate tonight to let me pass through with my maid; and within the days you have specified before you will surrender the city to our enemies, the LORD will rescue Israel by my hand." . . .

[9] Judith threw herself down prostrate, with ashes strewn upon her head, and wearing nothing over her sackcloth. While the incense was being offered in the temple of God in Jerusalem that evening, Judith prayed to the LORD with a loud voice: "LORD, God of my forefather Simeon! . . . O God, my God, hear me also, a widow. It is you who where the author of those events and of what preceded and followed them. The present, also, and the future you have planned. Whatever you devise comes into being; the things you decide on come forward and say, 'Here we are!' All your ways are in readiness, and your judgment is made with foreknowledge.

"Here are the Assyrians, a vast force, priding themselves on horse and rider, boasting of the power of their infantry, trusting in shield and spear, bow and sling. They do not know that

" 'You, the LORD, crush warfare;
  Lord is your name.'

"Shatter their strength in your might, and crush their force in your wrath; for they have resolved to profane your sanctuary, to defile the tent where your glorious name resides, and to overthrow with iron the horns of your altar. See their pride, and send forth your wrath upon their heads. Give me, a widow, the strong hand to execute my plan. With the guile of my lips, smite the slave together with the ruler, the ruler together with his servant; crush their pride by the hand of a woman.

"Your strength is not in numbers, nor does your power depend upon stalwart men; but you are the God of the lowly, the helper of the oppressed, the supporter of the weak, the protector of the forsaken, the savior of those without hope.

"Please, please, God of my forefather, God of the heritage of Israel, LORD of heaven and earth, Creator of the waters, King of all you have created, hear my prayer! Let my guileful speech bring wound and wale on those who have planned dire things against your covenant, your holy temple, Mount Zion, and the homes your children have inherited. Let your whole nation and all the tribes know clearly that you are the God of all power and might, and that there is no other who protects the people of Israel but you alone." . . .

[Then, through Judith's efforts, the Assyrians were routed.] . . .

[15] Judith led all Israel in this song of thanksgiving, and the people swelled this hymn of praise:

[16] "Strike up the instruments,
    a song to my God with timbrels,
    chant to the LORD with cymbals;
Sing to him a new song,
    exalt and acclaim his name.
For the LORD is God; he crushes warfare,
    and sets his encampment among his people;
    he snatched me from the hands of my
        persecutors. . . .

"Woe to the nations that rise against my people!
    the LORD Almighty will requite them;
    in the day of judgment he will punish them."

1 MACCABEES 9:44–46

Then Jonathan said to his companions, "Let us get up now and fight for our lives, for today is not like yesterday and the day before. The battle is before us, and behind us are the waters of the Jordan on one side, marsh and thickets on the other, and there is no way of escape. Cry out now to Heaven for deliverance from our enemies."

2 MACCABEES 8:1-4

Judas Maccabeus and his companions . . . implored the LORD to look kindly upon his people, who were being oppressed on all sides; to have pity on the temple, which was profaned by godless men; to have mercy on the city, which was being destroyed and about to be leveled to the ground; to hearken to the blood that cried out to him; to remember the criminal slaughter of innocent children and the blasphemies uttered against his name; and to manifest his hatred of evil.

2 CHRONICLES 20:9

When evil comes upon us, the sword of judgment, or pestilence, or famine, we will stand before this house and before you, for your name is in this house, and we will cry out to you in our affliction, and you will hear and save!

SCRIPTURE PASSAGES ON THE CRY OF JESUS

HEBREWS 5:7

In the days when he was in the flesh, he offered prayers and supplications with loud cries and tears to God, who was able to save him from death, and he was heard because of his reverence.

MARK 7:32–35

Some people brought him a deaf man who had a speech impediment and begged him to lay his hand on him. Jesus took him off by himself away from the crowd. He put his fingers into the man's ears and, spitting, touched his tongue; then he looked up to heaven and emitted a groan. He said to him, "*Ephphatha!*" (that is, "Be opened!") At once, the man's ears were opened; he was freed from the impediment, and began to speak plainly.

JOHN 11:35–44

Jesus began to weep, which caused the Jews to remark, "See how much he loved him!" But some said, "He opened the eyes of that blind man. Why could he not have done something to stop this man from dying?" Once again troubled in spirit, Jesus approached the tomb.

It was a cave with a stone laid across it. "Take away the stone," Jesus directed. Martha, the dead man's sister, said to him, "Lord, it has been four days now; surely there will be a stench!" Jesus replied, "Did I not assure you that if you believed you would see the glory of God displayed?" They then took away the stone and Jesus looked upward and said:

"Father, I thank you for having heard me.
I know that you always hear me
but I have said this for the sake of the crowd,
that they may believe that you sent me."

Having said this, he called loudly, "Lazarus, come out!" The dead man came out bound head and foot with linen strips, his face wrapped in a cloth. "Untie him," Jesus told them, "and let him go free."

MATTHEW 27:45-50

From noon onward, there was darkness over the whole land until midafternoon. Then toward midafternoon Jesus cried out in a loud tone, *"Eli, Eli, lema sabachthani?"*, that is, "My God, my God, why have you forsaken me?" This made some of the bystanders who heard it remark, "He is invoking Elijah!" Immediately one of them ran off and got a sponge. He soaked it in cheap wine, and sticking it on a reed, tried to make him drink. Meanwhile the rest said, "Leave him alone. Let's see whether Elijah comes to his rescue." Once again Jesus cried out in a loud voice, and then gave up his spirit.

MARK 15:34-37

At that time Jesus cried in a loud voice, *"Eloi, Eloi, lama sabachthani?"* which means, "My God, my God, why have you forsaken me?" A few of the bystanders who heard it remarked, "Listen! He is calling on Elijah!" Someone ran off, and soaking a sponge in sour wine, stuck it on a reed to try to make him drink. The man said, "Now let's see whether Elijah comes to take him down." Then Jesus, uttering a loud cry, breathed his last.

LUKE 23:46

Jesus uttered a loud cry and said,

"Father, into your hands I commend my spirit."

SCRIPTURE PASSAGES ON THE CRY
OF THE SONS AND DAUGHTERS OF GOD

GENESIS 4:8-10

Cain said to his brother Abel, "Let us go out in the field." When they were in the field, Cain attacked his brother Abel and killed him. Then the LORD asked Cain, "Where is your brother Abel?" He answered, "I do not know. Am I my brother's keeper?" The LORD then said: "What have you done! Listen: your brother's blood cries out to me from the soil!"

EXODUS 22:22-23

If ever you wrong them and they cry out to me, I will surely hear their cry. My wrath will flare up, and I will kill you with the sword; then your own wives will be widows, and your children orphans.

DEUTERONOMY 15:9

Be on your guard lest, entertaining the mean thought that the seventh year, the year of relaxation, is near, you grudge help to your needy kinsman and give him nothing; else he will cry to the LORD against you and you will be held guilty.

DEUTERONOMY 24:14-15

You shall not defraud a poor and needy hired servant, whether he be one of your own countrymen or one of the aliens who live in your communities. You shall pay him each day's wages before sundown on the day itself, since he is poor and looks forward to them. Otherwise he will cry to the LORD against you, and you will be held guilty.

JOB 29:12-13

For I [Job] rescued the poor who cried out for help,
    the orphans, and the unassisted;
The blessing of those in extremity came upon me.

JOB 38:41

Who provides nourishment for the ravens
    when their young ones cry out to God,
    and they rove abroad without food?

PSALM 18:5-7,17-20

The breakers of death surged round about me,
    the destroying floods overwhelmed me;
The cords of the nether world enmeshed me,
    the snares of death overtook me.
In my distress I called upon the LORD
    and cried out to my God;
From his temple he heard my voice,
    and my cry to him reached his ears. . . .

He reached out from on high and grasped me;
    he drew me out of the deep waters.
He rescued me from my mighty enemy
    and from my foes, who were too powerful for me.

They attacked me in the day of my calamity,
>   but the LORD came to my support.
He set me free in the open,
>   and rescued me, because he loves me.

PSALM 22:5-6

In you our fathers trusted;
>   they trusted, and you delivered them.
To you they cried and they escaped;
>   in you they trusted, and they were not put to
>   shame.

PSALM 28:1-2

To you, O LORD, I call;
>   O my Rock, be not deaf to me,
Lest, if you heed me not,
>   I become one of those going down into the pit.
Hear the sound of my pleading, when I cry to you,
>   lifting up my hands toward your holy shrine.

PSALM 30:9-13

To you, O LORD, I cried out;
>   with the LORD I pleaded:
"What gain would there be from my lifeblood,
>   from my going down into the grave?
Would dust give you thanks
>   or proclaim your faithfulness?
Hear, O LORD, and have pity on me;
>   O LORD, be my helper."

You changed my mourning into dancing;
you took off my sackcloth and clothed me with
gladness,
That my soul might sing praise to you without ceasing;
O LORD, my God, forever will I give you thanks.

PSALM 31:23

Once I said in my anguish,
"I am cut off from your sight";
Yet you heard the sound of my pleading
when I cried out to you.

PSALM 34:18-19

When the just cry out, the LORD hears them,
and from all their distress he rescues them.
The LORD is close to the brokenhearted;
and those who are crushed in spirit he saves.

PSALM 39:13

Hear my prayer, O LORD;
to my cry give ear;
to my weeping be not deaf!
For I am but a wayfarer before you,
a pilgrim like all my fathers.

PSALM 40:2-4

I have waited, waited for the LORD,
and he stooped toward me and heard my cry.

He drew me out of the pit of destruction,
    out of the mud of the swamp;
He set my feet upon a crag;
    he made firm my steps.
And he put a new song into my mouth,
    a hymn to our God.
Many shall look on in awe
    and trust in the LORD.

PSALM 88:2-3

O LORD, my God, by day I cry out;
    at night I clamor in your presence.
Let my prayer come before you;
    incline your ear to my call for help.

PSALM 102:2-21

O LORD, hear my prayer,
    and let my cry come to you.
Hide not your face from me
    in the day of my distress.
Incline your ear to me;
    in the day when I call, answer me speedily.
For my days vanish like smoke,
    and my bones burn like fire.
Withered and dried up like grass is my heart;
    I forget to eat my bread.
Because of my insistent sighing
    I am reduced to skin and bone.
I am like a desert owl;
    I have become like an owl among the ruins.
I am sleepless, and I moan;
    I am like a sparrow alone on the housetop.

All the day my enemies revile me;
     in their rage against me they make a curse of me.
For I eat ashes like bread
     and mingle my drink with tears,
Because of your fury and your wrath;
     for you lifted me up only to cast me down.
My days are like a lengthening shadow,
     and I wither like grass.

But you, O LORD, abide forever,
     and your name through all generations.
You will arise and have mercy on Zion,
     for it is time to pity her,
     for the appointed time has come.
For her stones are dear to your servants,
     and her dust moves them to pity.
And the nations shall revere your name, O LORD,
     and all the kings of the earth your glory.
When the LORD has rebuilt Zion
     and appeared in his glory;
When he has regarded the prayer of the destitute,
     and not despised their prayer.

Let this be written for the generation to come,
     and let his future creatures praise the LORD:
"The LORD looked down from his holy height,
     from heaven he beheld the earth,
To hear the groaning of the prisoners,
     to release those doomed to die."

PSALM 130:1-8

Out of the depths I cry to you, O LORD;
     LORD, hear my voice!

Let your ears be attentive
    to my voice in supplication:

If you, O LORD, mark iniquities,
    LORD, who can stand?
But with you is forgiveness,
    that you may be revered.

I trust in the LORD;
    my soul trusts in his word.
My soul waits for the LORD
    more than sentinels wait for the dawn.

More than sentinels wait for the dawn,
    let Israel wait for the LORD,
For with the LORD is kindness
    and with him is plenteous redemption;
And he will redeem Israel
    from all their iniquities.

PSALM 142:2-8

With a loud voice I cry out to the LORD;
    with a loud voice I beseech the LORD.
My complaint I pour out before him;
    before him I lay bare my distress.
When my spirit is faint within me,
    you know my path.

In the way along which I walk
    they have hid a trap for me.
I look to the right to see,
    but there is no one who pays me heed.
I have lost all means of escape;
    there is no one who cares for my life.

I cry out to you, O LORD;
    I say, "You are my refuge,
    my portion in the land of the living."
Attend to my cry,
    for I am brought low indeed.
Rescue me from my persecutors,
    for they are too strong for me.
Lead me forth from prison,
    that I may give thanks to your name.
The just shall gather around me
    when you have been good to me.

PROVERBS 21:13

He who shuts his ear to the cry of the poor
    will himself also call and not be heard.

SIRACH 51:9-10

So I raised my voice from the very earth,
    from the gates of the nether world, my cry.
I called out: O LORD, you are my father,
    you are my champion and my savior;
Do not abandon me in time of trouble,
    in the midst of storms and dangers.

ISAIAH 30:19

O people of Zion, who dwell in Jerusalem,
    no more will you weep;
He will be gracious to you when you cry out,
    as soon as he hears he will answer you.

ISAIAH 58:9-11

Then you shall call, and the LORD will answer,
  you shall cry for help, and he will say: Here I am!
If you remove from your midst oppression,
  false accusation and malicious speech;
If you bestow your bread on the hungry
  and satisfy the afflicted;
Then light shall rise for you in the darkness,
  and the gloom shall become for you like midday;
Then the LORD will guide you always
  and give you plenty even on the parched land.
He will renew your strength,
  and you shall be like a watered garden,
  like a spring whose water never fails.

LAMENTATIONS 3:46-59

All our enemies
  have opened their mouths against us;
Terror and the pit have been our lot,
  desolation and destruction;
My eyes run with streams of water
  over the downfall of the daughter of my people.

My eyes flow without ceasing,
  there is no respite,
Till the LORD from heaven
  looks down and sees.
My eyes torment my soul
  at the sight of all the daughters of my city.

Those who were my enemies without cause
  hunted me down like a bird;

They struck me down alive in the pit,
　　and sealed me in with a stone.
The waters flowed over my head,
　　and I said, "I am lost!"

I called upon your name, O LORD,
　　from the bottom of the pit;
You heard me call, "Let not your ear
　　be deaf to my cry for help!"
You came to my aid when I called to you;
　　you said, "Have no fear!"

You defended me in mortal danger,
　　you redeemed my life.
You see, O LORD, how I am wronged;
　　do me justice!

LAMENTATIONS 4:4

The tongue of the suckling cleaves
　　to the roof of its mouth in thirst;
The babes cry for food,
　　but there is no one to give it to them.

JONAH 2:2-8

From the belly of the fish Jonah said this prayer to the LORD, his God:

PSALM OF THANKSGIVING

Out of my distress I called to the LORD,
　　and he answered me;
From the midst of the nether world I cried for help,
　　and you heard my voice.

For you cast me into the deep, into the heart of the sea,
    and the flood enveloped me;
All your breakers and your billows
    passed over me.
Then I said, "I am banished from your sight!
    yet would I again look upon your holy temple."
The waters swirled about me, threatening my life;
    the abyss enveloped me;
    seaweed clung about my head.
Down I went to the roots of the mountains;
    the bars of the nether world
    were closing behind me forever,
But you brought my life up from the pit,
    O LORD, my God.
When my soul fainted within me,
    I remembered the LORD;
My prayer reached you
    in your holy temple.

MATTHEW 9:27–29

As Jesus moved on from there, two blind men came after him crying out, "Son of David, have pity on us!" When he got to the house, the blind men caught up with him. Jesus said to them, "Are you confident I can do this?" "Yes, Lord," they told him. At that he touched their eyes and said, "Because of your faith it shall be done to you."

MATTHEW 14:29–31

Peter got out of the boat and began to walk on the water, moving toward Jesus. But when he perceived how strong the wind was, becoming frightened, he began to sink and cried out, "Lord, save me!" Jesus at once stretched out his hand and caught him.

MATTHEW 15:22-28

It happened that a Canaanite woman living in that locality presented herself, crying out to him, "Lord, Son of David, have pity on me! My daughter is terribly troubled by a demon." He gave her no word of response. His disciples came up and began to entreat him, "Get rid of her. She keeps shouting after us." "My mission is only to the lost sheep of the house of Israel," Jesus replied. She came forward then and did him homage with the plea, "Help me, Lord!" But he answered, "It is not right to take the food of sons and daughters and throw it to the dogs." "Please, Lord," she insisted, "even the dogs eat the leavings that fall from their masters' tables." Jesus then said in reply, "Woman, you have great faith! Your wish will come to pass." That very moment her daughter got better.

ACTS 7:59-60

As Stephen was being stoned he could be heard praying, "Lord Jesus, receive my spirit." He fell to his knees and cried out in a loud voice, "Lord, do not hold this sin against them." And with that he died.

ROMANS 8:15

You did not receive a spirit of slavery leading you back into fear, but a spirit of adoption through which we cry out, "Abba!" (that is, "Father").

ROMANS 8:22-24

Yes, we know that all creation groans and is in agony even until now. Not only that, but we ourselves, although we have the Spirit as first fruits, groan inwardly while we await the redemption of our bodies. In hope we were saved.

GALATIANS 4:6-7

The proof that you are sons is the fact that God has sent forth into our hearts the spirit of his Son which cries out "Abba!" ("Father!") You are no longer a slave but a son! And the fact that you are a son makes you an heir, by God's design.

JAMES 5:1-4

As for you, you rich, weep and wail over your impending miseries. Your wealth has rotted, your fine wardrobe has grown moth-eaten, your gold and silver have corroded, and their corrosion shall be a testimony against you; it will devour your flesh like a fire. See what you have stored up for yourselves against the last days. Here, crying aloud, are the wages you withheld from the farmhands who harvested your fields. The cries of the harvesters have reached the ears of the Lord of hosts.

REVELATION 21:1-4

Then I saw new heavens and a new earth. The former heavens and the former earth had passed away, and the sea was no longer. I also saw a new Jerusalem, the holy city, coming down out of heaven from God, beautiful as a bride prepared to meet her husband. I heard a loud voice from the throne cry out: "This is God's dwelling among men. He shall dwell with them and they shall be his people and he shall be their God who is always with them. He shall wipe every tear from their eyes, and there shall be no more death or mourning, crying out or pain, for the former world has passed away."

Scripture Index

OLD TESTAMENT

NEW TESTAMENT